Night of the Frogs
Sautee and Nacoochee

Robert Manns

Trees,
So small a thank you
for all your work.

Bob

Writers Club Press
San Jose New York Lincoln Shanghai

Night of the Frogs & Sautee and Nacoochee

Published by Writers Club Press
an imprint of iUniverse.com, Inc.

For information address:
iUniverse.com, Inc.
620 North 48th Street
Suite 201
Lincoln, NE 68504-3467
www.iuniverse.com

ISBN: 0-595-00292-7

Printed in the United States of America

CONTENTS

Night of the Frogs

Sautee and Nacoochee

Night of the Frogs

A History Play

Robert Manns

NIGHT OF THE FROGS was first produced in 1973 by DeKalb County Parks and Recreation at Callanwolde Art Center in Atlanta. The part of Tituba was played by Georgia Allen in the outdoor theater on the grounds. Several of the opening nights, the meadow scene was serenaded by two non-equity Screech owls high in oaks above the stage which certainly added a propitious touch.

But because my agent of the time dreaded the idea of working for the play in New York due to the existence of Mr. Miller's play, it went to the bottom of the author's works until this publication. I firmly believe it deserves better.

The Author

CAST OF CHARACTERS

Tituba, about forty, powerful.

Stoughton, fifty, heavy, fiery.

Parris, a meek man, superstitious and servile. Fortyish.

Rebecca Nurse

Sarah Good, large, in her fifties.

William Good, smaller, in his late fifties.

Burroughs, a minister.

Robert Calef, wealthy Boston merchant.

John Proctor

Elizabeth Proctor

Abigail Williams, stiff and humorless.

Betty Parris

Ann Putnam

Governor Phips

Wilfred Hogg, short, lean.

Bayles

Mobley

Mary

Two Girls, in the courtroom.

Sarah Osburne, a sadly defenseless woman of her late thirties.

ACT ONE

(1)

Black night in Salem Village, in 1692. Reverend Samuel Parris' meadow, eloquently spoken for by giant bullfrogs. A pale moonlight lays weakly over the damp ground and no other sound but the frogs is heard. The concert of the amphibians continues until ENTER TITUBA, and behind her BETTY, ABIGAIL, and ANN PUTNAM, all entering the years of puberty. Tituba, half Carib and half Negro, is about forty.

TITUBA: I prophesy
      A ram's blood,
      Earthen flood,
      Face of God
      In Salem mud.

ABIGAIL: (*whispered*) There, you hear, Ann Putnam? She foretells.

ANN: (*whispered*) I hear it.

ABIGAIL: (*whispered*) Isn't it grand? She is from Barbados. My uncle, Reverend Parris, says she is Carib and Negro. He brought her back with him his last trip there. She is matron to Betty and me since Mrs. Parris died.

BETTY: Must you tell everything, Abigail?

ABIGAIL: I do believe Betty is jealous because I dance best.

ANN: Do you dance?

ABIGAIL: Yes, we have a maypole, too. And will see things you've never seen. Someday, she says, we will have a Christmas, and drink ale till we're drunk.

BETTY: And see witches!

ABIGAIL: And watch them drink blood!

BETTY: And consort with the devil!

ANN: It's black magic!

ABIGAIL: Yes, and fun. Tituba is versed in it all. She makes a night of it, and so shall we.

TITUBA: (*Full Voice*)
        Tituba see the meadow rise
        Rise and fall, like Satan's belly.
        He breathe the sweat of our bodies.
        But virgin, no; he Tituba take.
        Then in grass, fill her up with frogs!
        She will gives suck to polliwogs!

ANN: (*whispered*) You hear, Betty Parris?

BETTY: She would consort.

ABIGAIL: Call it what you like. I know what she would do to get her
　　　　frogs. She has courage.

ANN: She called the devil.

ABIGAIL: To draw him out. Listen.

ANN: I am afraid.

ABIGAIL: You've seen nothing to be afraid of. Listen.
　　　　(*End of whispering*)

TITUBA: I cry you, old man, send me sign
　　　　Make gold bird rise, find me poppet
　　　　Bleeding needles, make the hound howl!
　　　　Strange, strange is your silence tonight.
　　　　We will have dancing, then, mind you.
　　　　Dance, young legs, let your spirits fly;
　　　　Let the old man be your ally.
　　　　Yes, dance. What, won't you move?

ABIGAIL: (*whispered*) Come, Ann, I'll show you.

ANN: It is forbidden.

ABIGAIL: Look, look, at Tituba, and follow me.

ANN: But where is the maypole? How do you dance without a maypole?

ABIGAIL: There is none. Follow Betty; look, she dances!

ANN: I cannot. Oh, I cannot. I will not defy my God.

ABIGAIL: It is a silly rule. God bids us dance to draw out his enemies. You will have to follow me, then. (*They all dance, Tituba first, Ann Putnam joining reluctantly.*) (*End of whispering*)

TITUBA: Tituba
Meditate
Advocate
Actuate
Allocate
Aggravate!

Tituba
Congregate
Detonate
Decorate
Captivate
Celebrate!

She never fall! Tituba all! Tituba queen!
Tituba feel the red man in her spleen! (*The girls scream*)

Tituba
Invocate
Titillate
Propagate
Tabulate
Tolerate

She
Undulate
Satiate
Saturate

Generate
She create!

She never fall! Tituba all! Tituba queen!
Fear of God keep Tituba clean! (*The girls shout agreement*)
Betty, what d'you see?

BETTY: (*She has stopped*) I see a yellow bird!
(*Pointing*) There!

ABIGAIL: I see it! There is a black one with it! Gone, like that.

TITUBA: You have eyes to see light and dark.
It was a crow and meadowlark.

ANN: I thought I saw one of them.

ABIGAIL: Ann saw one! That is a good sign; do you think so, Tituba?

TITUBA: A sign of pure at heart. It is.

ABIGAIL: Which one did you see?

ANN: Why, I saw the yellow breast of the meadowlark, I think.

BETTY: She saw mine, then. Mine was yellow underneath!

ABIGAIL: She saw Betty's.

ANN: I saw Betty's.

TITUBA: I saw Abigail's. Signs are out.
  Devil is astir hereabout.
  The croaking of night things do break
  When threatened by the quick and coiled snake!
  Watch, therefore, your signs; he is near.
  All sound is quit, turned off! He's here!
  (*The frogs stop*)

BETTY: (*Wails*) Ohhh—

ABIGAIL: Who is it, sir? I do not know you.

ANN: Abby, who is it?

ANN: Where is he? I see nothing. There is nothing but night around us.
  You told me you had a maypole, there was none.

ABIGAIL: You are not looking with your eyes, Ann Putnam.
  See there on the low bough of that oak, swinging his legs. You saw
  Betty's yellow bird; what blinds you now?

ANN: The dark does, Abby.

ABIGAIL: He is coming down!

TITUBA: Join hands now.

BETTY: He fell; he will be angry.

TITUBA: Join hands, I tell you.

ANN: I do see something.

TITUBA: Hand in hand is formula for safety,
      Strength, and gives to the mind asperity,
      A surface mountainous, cragged and rough,
      Against which serpent devils cry enough.
      Hold, name yourself!

ABIGAIL: He speaks.

TITUBA: And says nothing. It's he, sure.

ABIGAIL: Yet he tries, Tituba.

TITUBA: Name your legions, Devil, divulge your friends.
      Tell what witch it is who at night ascends
      And, throwing sticks at Tituba's kitchen,
      Rouses her Barbados anger and chagrin.
      For these things done are stoutly magical
      And are named in Salem as heretical.

ABIGAIL: Do you see him, Ann?

ANN: I do, I do.

ABIGAIL: Look there at Betty.

ANN: Why, she looks sick.

ABIGAIL: It is hard on her. She will not weather it.

TITUBA: Name, man, or begone! I say begone!

ABIGAIL: Name or go.

ANN: Abigail, Betty is ill.

ABIGAIL: He choked me. Tituba, take his hands off me. I am being
    choked!

TITUBA: Lucifer, avoid, in God's name avoid
    You, this Abigail's soul is unalloyed,
    Unmixed and unmistakably her God's!
    Shift, shift! Your reason's made of moist dungclods!
    I say off and away, unhand and go!
    You are evil's gigolo! *(The frogs begin again.)*

ABIGAIL: Dear Tituba, I thank you. He has let me go now.
    Ann Putnam, what's with Betty on the ground?

ANN: She has fainted.

TITUBA: *(Picking Betty up)*
                Oh, my Lord
    Is in his heaven,
    Keeping safe my little wren.
    Little bird, little wren,
    Fallen from her nest again.
    Home it is then.

ABIGAIL: Well, aren't you going to ask me who I saw?

TITUBA: No, ma'am, home it is now.

ABIGAIL: I saw who throws sticks at Tituba's kitchen.

TITUBA: You could not.

ABIGAIL: I did, and went to give her name—but could not for his choking
    me.

TITUBA: You know the witch?

ABIGAIL: I do.

TITUBA: You could not.

ABIGAIL: I do, I tell you!

TITUBA: Did the witch fly? She must take flight.

ABIGAIL: Yes, she flew.

TITUBA: Well, speak
    On.

ABIGAIL: She flew to the aid of Betty. *(She laughs, enjoining Ann to
    laugh with her, hoping to make an ally and frighten Tituba.)*

TITUBA: There are times too early and times too late
    For jest and mockery to postulate
    Much of sense or any of wisdom
    Beyond the humdrum or the wearisome.
    Now is too late. We go home.

ABIGAIL: Tituba is a spoiler, isn't she, Ann?

ANN: Yes, and I saw her fly, too.

ABIGAIL: Good for you!

TITUBA: Saw who fly?

ANN: I saw you go over—

TITUBA: Forbear! Tituba will carry an armful
          Of bodies home! One to put abed,
          Some to bury.

ANN: It was a joke only.

TITUBA: Burn it; are we ready?

ABIGAIL: Yes, ready.

TITUBA: Now, Ann Putnam, that you are new with us
          Is signature of your innocence.
          Yet does your innocence have mockery
          In it. Mockery, jest and pointed wit
          Are too profound for spirited children
          And danger signs to kindly Tituba.
          I reveal my craft and you joke with me.
          You too, Abigail. It is much unkind.
          I do take it ill and would have you both
          Now drop those private, worthless, grinnings
          To the liquid ground and bravely lose them
          For all time as one would watch a prized coin,
          Ventured for the skipping of a wooded stream,
          Get thrown, dip and sink, even to the loss
          Of its owner. Look to it. I will not have
          Your smirks.

ANN: I am sorry, Tituba.

ABIGAIL: I, too.

TITUBA: I tell you, think so with less deceit
        Than you speak. Nor must any unkept word
        Be sprung upon the casual listener
        Or careworn parent of what we do here.
        We do no more than what you wish to do.
        My charms and spells are secret, not for hire,
        Not for inquiry and not for jesting.
        As Betty was your trusted confidant,
        My first pupil, we are leagued through her
        To secrecy. The Reverend Parris,
        Her good father, discoursed in church on Hell,
        Satan, evil's flowers and the brimstone way
        Till Betty, curious, I informed her
        On my ways. I reveal what is suspect.
        I will have my curiosity,
        Not linger with another's. But what is mine
        Is mine, keep you tight what is rightly yours,
        Now. No word on it.

ABIGAIL: I will.

ANN: And I will.

TITUBA: Swear on it.

ABIGAIL: I swear!

ANN: I swear!

TITUBA: By the
          Good Lord.

ABIGAIL: I swear in his name!

ANN: By my sweet Lord, I swear!

TITUBA: Be truthful now; you have sworn!

ABIGAIL: I am truthful!

ANN: I am truthful!

TITUBA: Tituba has a horror of you both.
          A seed's threat is in its aftergrowth. Come.

(2)

Reverend Parris' home, the parsonage. Its living room. Parris is sitting in a chair by candles reading his Bible. Enter ABIGAIL.

PARRIS: My house, my dog, are all asleep, Abby;
      Where were you?

ABIGAIL: Out, sir. Good evening to you.

PARRIS: That's a general answer.
      Tell me, what continent were you on, then?

ABIGAIL: What mean you, sir?

PARRIS: Why, I mean to have an answer less shaped
      By generality and more specific.
      Were you in Salem or in Beverly,
      Marblehead or Andover? Answer to it.

ABIGAIL: Sir, I never go out of Salem Village.

PARRIS: Oh? Where were you, then, in Salem Village?

ABIGAIL: Here in Salem, Reverend Parris.

PARRIS: Where, I want to know? Do not beguile me;
      Answer!

ABIGAIL: I was with Betty and Ann Putnam.

PARRIS: Yes, if you were some years older
           I would accept that as a woman's answer
           And rankle at the simple hit and miss
           Of ordinary conversation. Come,
           I mean to have it.

ABIGAIL: Dear sir, we walked in many places and I can name them all to you if I must. We walked to the meeting house, past John Proctor's, by Reverend Donovan's church and back to your own.

PARRIS: Leaving nothing out?

ABIGAIL: I think not.

PARRIS: My orchard, mind you? No strolling there?

ABIGAIL: Oh, yes, briefly. I did forget the orchard.

PARRIS: Well, and with Ann Putnam, did you say?

ABIGAIL: True, sir, and Betty, who is in her bed—having come back earlier.

PARRIS: And Ann gone home, too, no doubt, is that it?

ABIGAIL: Yes.

PARRIS: All at peace. Salem passes into sleep
           Then, impervious to shame, immune to sin.
           Again, another night, she will navigate
           Her starry and celestial course with God.
           This is as you put it.

ABIGAIL: How else to put it?

PARRIS: Open the door
        And let in Ann Putnam. We'll see how else.

ABIGAIL: But she is gone home.

PARRIS: Lie no more! She does listen at that door.
        (ENTER ANN PUTNAM, BEING LET IN BY ABIGAIL)
        Now truth being still in season here
        We will disengage from machination
        And go a course more natural and ripe.
        The time, girl, is nature in her patient wait
        Upon fidelity to form. Who made
        Your company?

ABIGAIL: We three girls.

PARRIS: And? There were more. Come, now.

ABIGAIL: Tituba.

PARRIS: Who now puts Betty in her bed above,
        I surmise, having entered at the back.
        I do walk in my own orchard sometimes.

ABIGAIL: Reverend Parris, sir!

PARRIS: Oh, did you not know God is everywhere?

ABIGAIL: What did you see?

PARRIS: I saw you dance, and withdrew in disgust.
        Your punishments will follow on the morrow
        With alacrity, and publication
        Of your sins will hang in the meeting house.
        Even as you come from my own home
        Will this be done. Thanks be to God my wife
        Was not here to see it.

ABIGAIL: You should not have left, but seen it all, then.

PARRIS: -   Well, well, what all?

ANN: Abigail!

ABIGAIL: Surely, Ann, we must confess it totally. Uncle, Tituba has
        revealed to us, and we were into witchcraft this night.

PARRIS: How into? And I warn, use good caution.

ABIGAIL: I was attacked!

PARRIS: By whom attacked, and proceed with vigil
        Over your thoughts, and good government
        Of your tongue, for witchcraft is heretical
        In highest puritan theocracy,
        Punishable with our strictest laws
        And damned in God's eyes and by his canon.

ABIGAIL: I would not have her name again upon my lips.

PARRIS: Well, you will; I would hear it and clear.

ABIGAIL: Sir, it will go hard on this house if I name.

PARRIS: On this house? Witchcraft here? You concoct lies
        From imagination, girl. Separate,
        I beg you, truth from untruth or, on my word,
        And before God, this hand will design
        On your backside clear division of them.
        Now, who is it hurt you?

ABIGAIL: Uncle, take heed.

PARRIS: Name or confess
        To hell yourself.

ABIGAIL: *(Screams)*

ANN: *(Screams)*

ABIGAIL: Tituba called on Satan who sent her spirit choking me. I
        saw it; Ann saw it, and my neck is still bruised. It is Tituba
        who is the witch at Salem, as Glover is of Boston, and in
        your own house, in this parsonage, below God's roof. Is it
        not so, Ann?

ANN: It is so, sir.

PARRIS: It cannot be, in my house.
        Fetch Tituba.

(EXIT ABIGAIL)
           Now, Ann Putnam, how were you
        Involved with witchcraft?

ANN: Oh, it is wond'rous, sir. Betty asked me and I asked my
mother let me come. She said if there are witches in Salem,
they must be found out and bade me go. I have seen the at-
tacking of Abigail. I cried out for him to stop but he kept on.
When Tituba told him stop, he stopped.

PARRIS: Just like that, did he?

ANN: Yes, Reverend Parris.

PARRIS: How did she control the act, if you please?

ANN: I do not know, sir.

(ENTER ABIGAIL AND TITUBA)

PARRIS: How is my daughter?

TITUBA: She sleeps peacefully, sir.

PARRIS: Shape the devil now.

TITUBA: I do not know him, sir.

PARRIS: Think, I mean, not know. I will ask what you know
In my good time. What are your ideas on him?

TITUBA: Well, sir, he is fat if he is a glutton.

PARRIS: Is he glutton?

TITUBA: I do believe so.

PARRIS: Excellent, some thinkers feature him as lean,
　　　　Too. What of that?

TITUBA:　　　　　　Lean in the beginning, sir.
　　　　But being glutton he could not stay lean long,
　　　　For, feeding on the wicked in the world,
　　　　He got big of belly and does now boast
　　　　A great paunch. You say in Sunday sermon
　　　　There is much sin afoot; if sin be his food,
　　　　Then, his plate kept full, glutton will eat,
　　　　All things being savory, and grow stout.
　　　　Or so I think. It's thinking tells me so.

PARRIS: Woe, I ever sailed to Barbados!

ANN: It is blasphemy!

ABIGAIL: Yes, Ann, it is. A description made to confuse, and make
　　　　us liars all. We know the devil's shape.

PARRIS: Why did Nehemiah's cow froth and die
　　　　One week ago, woman? Answer you that.

TITUBA: That foolish cow ate of jimson weed, sir,
　　　　Poisoned nightshade.

PARRIS:　　　　　　Base mockery is here!
　　　　Subterfuge is wicked, concealment sin,
　　　　By every precept. The sign is on you
　　　　For a witch, Tituba! Will you confess it?

TITUBA: Sir, I am no witch. I mock as they mocked.
　　　　I do suggest they took our fun too much
　　　　To heart.

PARRIS:　　　Fun, you say? You say to me fun?

TITUBA: Yes, fun. Believing what one wants for sport.

PARRIS: Fun and sport. Every word's a new growth!
　　　　Our Christ has suffered himself for sport?

ABIGAIL: I was choked for sport? *(Abigail cries out)*

ANN: *(Cries out)*

TITUBA: Yes, for sport!

ABIGAIL: *(Falls to her knees)* You are hurting me, Tituba. Let go,
　　　　oh, let me go!

ANN: Let her go, you demon!

TITUBA:　　　　　　　　　　Tituba does nothing!

ABIGAIL & ANN: Tituba does nothing!

TITUBA: Tituba is innocent!

ABIGAIL & ANN: Tituba is innocent!

TITUBA:　　　　　　　　　　Oh, the fool!

ABIGAIL & ANN: Oh, the fool!

PARRIS: It is enough. It is enough, I say.
          Release these children, you blackened harlot,
          And confess yourself to witchery.
          For demon of the underworld you are.
          Liberate them and submit you to it.

TITUBA: *(Capitulating, going to her knees)*
          Oh, dear Lord, and my Reverend Master,
          I am no witch, I am not bad.
          Tituba's tongue is winter-clad,
          Too heavy to fend against this massacre.
          (The children resume natural aspects)

PARRIS: By my vision, it is witchery plain
          And all too simple, but I'll discuss it.
          I will go to Boston this same night,
          Seek out our deputy Governor
          And return him here by daybreak.
          His good experience in these matters
          Will direct us. Meanwhile, witch Tituba,
          Tonight you sleep afield, molest not this house.
          Return here early for your judgement.
          Turn out, and you hold no more traffic
          With the Devil.

TITUBA: Master Parris—

PARRIS: So now,
          On my command. And mind be back indoors
          With the first sun. If I am absent,
          You will wait in the yard. Now go. Now go.

(EXIT TITUBA)

Well, dear Abigail and Ann, off to bed
With Betty and bar tight your windows.
Tomorrow, Salem will be scourged and cleansed
Of Lucifer's disciples and reason reign
Again. To bed now.

(EXIT ABIGAIL & ANN. PARRIS DONS A COAT, TAKES CROP FROM A PEG AND EXITS. HE FAILS TO CLOSE THE DOOR FIRMLY. IT GLIDES WIDE OPEN AND WE HEAR THE CROAKING OF THE FROGS THROUGH THE DIM-OUT, DURING THE BLACKOUT, AND UNTIL THE MORNING LIGHT AGAIN LIGHTS THE SAME SCENE.

MORNING LIGHT. SOUND OF HORSES BEING REINED TO A STOP. ENTER STOUGHTON, WHO IS DEPUTY GOVERNOR OF MASSA-CHUSETTS, AN ORDAINED MINISTER AND HEAD OF A PARISH; THEN ROBERT CALEF, A BOSTON MERCHANT; AND LASTLY PARRIS.)

PARRIS: My door open?
    I shut it tight. Excuse me, I must see
    To the safety of my small charges.

(EXIT PARRIS)

STOUGHTON: An open parapet, Mister Calef,
    In a fort besieged is poor defense
    Against the heathen Indian, not so?
    What might Satan pour through such a crevice?

CALEF: What about the night air, Mr. Stoughton? *(Closes the door.)*

STOUGHTON: He might. He might just pass in humid air.

CALEF: Well, you have humanized the devil, lately.

STOUGHTON: I have? How so?

CALEF: If he passes air, sir.

STOUGHTON: In Boston I acceded to your wish
        To come with me to Salem witnessing
        These proceedings at their origins,
        In the bud and at first hand, sir.
        I know you are doubtful of Glover's guilt
        In Boston. But do not shackle me
        With your opinions till you have seen it all
        And then act according to your will.
        You are new to Satan, while I am not.
        I have deposed and hanged more witches
        In this State than you have heard of,
        And know the signs of their coming
        Like I know my hand. But do, I warn you,
        Court caution, sanitize your comments.

CALEF: I will not offend again without cause.

STOUGHTON: Nor, I beg you, take offense, either,
        Because, I tell you plain, you are my parish's
        Most valued member.

CALEF: True, the richest.

STOUGHTON: And your shipping is needed in Boston.

CALEF: As Deputy Governor you have the right
To act for the law. I stand rebuked.

STOUGHTON: And do not chafe?

CALEF: And do not chafe, sir.

STOUGHTON: Good.

(ENTER PARRIS)

PARRIS: Not a wen on them. No excrescences,
Not a mark. No fear in their little hearts
Even. Our Father has watched over them.
Do take off your coats, gentlemen, and wash.
Make my house yours and do quite as you please.
I appreciate your quick attention
To my cry in the night; we will nip this
Early at its root now. Do wash, do wash.
The girls will be down momently.
(The men remove their coats and wash.)
But what broke my door open? And Tituba
Not yet here, either.

CALEF: Mr. Stoughton,
What would you do for a few hours sleep?

STOUGHTON: I would take up farming, Mr. Calef,
If I thought the sleep hours could be regular.
There is no counting on them in politics.

PARRIS: Would you care to sleep before seeing the girls,
        Judge Stoughton?

STOUGHTON: No, we will see them now, sir.

PARRIS: That open door does import something sure.

STOUGHTON: It is not the main sign we will look for,
        Though. The accusations are important
        Since we know the Devil cannot assume
        The form of innocent inhabitants.
        Those whose shapes infest the air are guilty
        Ipso facto. He has picked and trained these
        To flourish his doctrine, rend our good faith.
        Anyone who flies, keeps toads, frogs, poppets,
        Sends up birds, brings down illness, accident
        And death is damned and sooner hanged the better.
        This is our main evidence, product
        Of our latest learning on the subject
        And immune to disputation, in my eye.

PARRIS: It is a blessing to have you here, sir,
        For guidance in the matter.

(ENTER ABIGAIL, BETTY, AND ANN)

STOUGHTON: These are the girls?

PARRIS: Abigail, Ann and Betty, here are friends
        From Boston: Judge Stoughton, Mister Calef.

THE GIRLS: How d'you do, sir.

STOUGHTON: I have some questions of you. You have named
   A witch. God damns all liars, this you know.
   Do you know it?

THE GIRLS: Oh, yes, sir.

STOUGHTON: Then why do you lie? *(The girls attempt to*
   guess the Judge's paradox, Parris moves uneasily.)

ABIGAIL: We do not lie, sir.

STOUGHTON: I say you do.

ABIGAIL: No, sir.

STOUGHTON: Yes, and say you persecute
   This woman out of malice.

BETTY: No, no, I love Tituba, sir. She has taught me everything.

STOUGHTON: Oh, such as?

BETTY: To see things.

STOUGHTON: Like what, pray? Be specific, if you can.

BETTY: Shapes. Shapes flying.

STOUGHTON: Well, and who flies here in Salem Village?

ABIGAIL: Tituba flew last night. I saw it.

ANN: I saw it.

STOUGHTON: *(To Betty)* Did you see it?

BETTY: I fainted, sir.

STOUGHTON: Has this Tituba
    A mole or a devil's teat that shows itself?

BETTY: On her neck, a thing—

STOUGHTON: Where do you dance with her? I hear you dance.

BETTY: At the frog pond, sir.

STOUGHTON: What did you say, my child?

BETTY: There on the floor back of you—is a frog! *(Hysteria,*
    screams from the girls)

ABIGAIL: Tituba!

ANN: Tituba.

STOUGHTON: *(To Parris)* Where is that woman?!

*(ENTER TITUBA, POUNDING OPEN THE CLOSED DOOR, HAG-
GARD, DISHEVELED, HEAD DOWN. LOOKING HIDEOUSLY THE
WITCH—AND BELLOWING TO THE FLOOR)*

TITUBA: Tituba here! *(Pause)*

STOUGHTON: Come to me, woman approach me. Come here. *(She does*
   slowly & ponderously)
   It looks bad for you in Salem; what d' you say?
   I want reply! Silence is confession!
   The time is not a pretty one, or hour
   Fortunate. Puritan theocracy
   Is climaxed past its flower if you prevail.
   Lift your head to me, woman.
   (She does, to the horror of all. Her face is bloody.
   Stoughton recoils, the children scream.)

                    Cleanse your horror!
   Go make yourself clean, hag. It is a sight
   To fright the damned, the dead, and memory of both.
   Wash, wash! Sweet God have pity on your children.

(EXIT TITUBA ATTENDED BY PARRIS AND CALEF)

(The children crying)
Now be ardent, robust, energetic
In your purpose. Be compassionate
But truthful. Be brave. God has signaled you
To a task would jar the nerve of owls.
You must erase this town of witchcraft.
Who else afflicts you? Who conjures? Who spites?
Name me names! Who flies? Who bears false witness?
Who does adulterate? I must have names.
Think on it and then be relieved. God's will
Be done.

(Abigail stamps and crushes the frog)

VOICE OF TITUBA: I will confess, confess. I saw
Sarah Good and Sarah Osburne fly. Yes,
I saw them over Mister Metcalf's barn.
Flying. *(Wails)* They flew.

THE GIRLS: Goody Good and Goody Osburne.

VOICE OF TITUBA: Tituba innocent. *(Wails to the end*
of the scene)

THE GIRLS: Goody Good and Goody Osburne. *(etc. etc.)*

STOUGHTON: It is given to me to preside here,
Till sin and wickedness disappear.
Come, Parris, we must ride for warrants
To put an end to such disconsolance.

(3)

The grounds behind the parsonage. Late the same day. Present are Stoughton, Calef, Parris, Tituba (irons on her wrists), and three men of Salem Village, Wilfred Hogg, Bayles, and Mobley.

HOGG: Yup, serving the warrant on Osburne was easy. She took it like a good woman ought, got 'er things t'gether, stepped into the wagon of 'er own accord, and I shackled 'er. That was it. But Sarah Good, she's a witch for sure, the dog faced ol' hag. Unseat me from m' horse, near broke m' back fallin' to the road, and shooed away the horse which I never yet found. As I am made sheriff I will have her.

BAYLES: A pimple on her ass for an old hag, Wilfred, we'll catch the witch. And find your mare, too.

MOBLEY: Sssh your tongue, Bayles, not a stone's throw away from Parris' parsonage y' are.

BAYLES: Well, I don't hanker witches, Mobley.

HOGG: Sneak me a little beer while we wait, Bayles.

BAYLES: Keep it low. *(From his saddle beside him, he passes Hogg a beer.)* Mobley?

MOBLEY: Kindly of y', Bayles. *(Mobley takes a beer.)*

BAYLES: I hope to soon be on with it.

TITUBA: Right, let us get on with it. Why delay?! *(She is alone, shackled to the cart.)*

STOUGHTON: Mister Parris, How soon can we begin
      For the strumpet and witch, Sarah Good?

PARRIS: Why, I think everything is ready now.
      I will have the men saddle the horses. *(He goes to Hogg,*
      Bayles and Mobley and—)

(EXIT PARRIS AND WILFRED HOGG)

STOUGHTON: I came here less for hare and hounds, Calef,
      Than for justice, but if we must ride
      For equity, obedience and law
      I have a good leg and quick spur, I think.

CALEF: Why is the woman to be brought with us;
      Do we need company? She will be roughed
      In the cart.

STOUGHTON: It takes a witch to catch one.
      She is our hound. Why was her face so torn
      This morning? Did she explain it to you?

CALEF: Yes, sir. She confided that in Barbados
      Arrests were sometimes made of voodoo priests
      Who circumspectly disfigured their bodies
      And impaired their being so their accusers
      Were, on no account, denied full pleasure
      Of their accusations. With a hand knife
      She carved humiliation from hair line

Into jawbone. She was conscience-stricken,
Angry and afraid.

STOUGHTON: Wench and strumpet. Witch,
No less, and no more, either. Voodoo priests.
Voodoo priests, eh? Did you note her frog form?
She was present with us from the start,
And knew her guilt firsthand. She is a witch.

CALEF: The frog, poor Rana temporaria,
Who mashed his guts?

STOUGHTON: The girl, Abigail.
And as soon done, the uncouth witch confessed.

CALEF: No, as soon told by Parris she would hang.

STOUGHTON: Why, I heard it, hard on the destruction
Of the frog.

CALEF: And I, hard on threat of hanging.

STOUGHTON: Now, now, what do you mean, Mister Calef?

CALEF: For meaning, sir, I lose. Meaning is made
Of sense for me, and nonsense abounds here
To awesome distraction. The wood prevents
Clear vision of a tree to hang meaning on.

STOUGHTON: And the behavior, then, of Sarah Good?
This is nonsense, putting us to hunt her!

CALEF: No, I will confess that does make good sense.

STOUGHTON: It does convict her, man.

CALEF: True, sir, if caught.

STOUGHTON: If caught? You do underestimate me,
          Mister Calef. I never came so far
          To be eluded. I do not chase the wind
          Of my imagination, fantasy,
          Or vain conceit, but seek a warmer blood
          Of real and actual and living stuff,
          The damned witch, and when I hunt I do find game.
          Now put that hellhag's cart behind a horse,
          You men, do it, and let us get going.
          We neglect law and shame God in our dalliance.
          Courses are for taking before they change
          And history overwhelms us with its own.
          To horse, Mister Calef, we are moving.

(The cart is drawn off by Bayles and Mobley and all.)

(EXIT)

(4)

A field. Sarah Good, stout and strong, looking seventy but actually aged closer to forty-eight or fifty, sits on a large rock, smoking her pipe. Her face is leathery and lined, her teeth broken, brown or gone. Her hair is filthy and stuck in as many directions as the compass has. She smokes and thinks seriously. She mumbles half-spoken thoughts, adjusts her rags, mumbles.

(ENTER WILLIAM, HER HUSBAND)

WILLIAM: They come for y', Sar'.

SARAH: Damn 'em for their witches.

WILLIAM: Whole mighty crowd. Horses, carts, the black Tituba.

SARAH: Let 'em; a mighty fortress is our God. Haw!

WILLIAM: Oh, my heaven, woman. Why did you scare off the sheriff's horse?

SARAH: I could not scare off the sheriff, is why, William. You sit.

WILLIAM: Oh, Lord.

SARAH: Sit. *(He does not.)*

WILLIAM: Such an army they send out.

SARAH: Need 'em all, they do, every man, every horse. Sarah's foul.

WILLAIM: Look, wife, make your peace to 'em. Learn the commandments.

SARAH: I'm a sloven hag, I cannot learn.

WILLIAM: I could teach 'em to you.

SARAH: I learn them not, though. I'm a hag.

WILLIAM: I have always labored for y', Sar'—

SARAH: True.

WILLIAM: I could teach the commandments.

SARAH: I could not learn.

WILLIAM: You must redeem somehow.

SARAH: I run. Damn 'em for their witches.

WILLIAM: *(He sits.)* I do love y', woman. I found y' in Boston Town and I have labored for y' since.

SARAH: No more.

WILLIAM: Oh yes, if y' let be.

SARAH: I'm a hag, witch, no.

WILLIAM: You are obstinate. Mend with me.

SARAH: They are, they are.

WILLIAM: True, and powerful, too. But mend, woman.

SARAH: *(She gives him a playful, cubbish, feel of his hair, near gone.)* Y' know Sarah.

WILLIAM: Proud wench.

SARAH: It's best, I think.

WILLIAM: Maybe, tho' pride is not of the Bible, Sar'.

SARAH: Haw!

WILLIAM: It's pride take y' from me.

SARAH: That's sure, theirs.

WILLIAM: Y' be with child?

SARAH: I do, William.

WILLIAM: God be with y' both, then.

SARAH: *(She spits enormously.)*

WILLIAM: Come now. Make to Andover.

SARAH: *(Standing)* Which way is 't?

WILLIAM: Follow the firs.

SARAH: Is that the firthest way? *(Pause. She laughs ecstatically.)*

(EXIT WILLIAM)

(She laughs.)

(EXIT SARAH GOOD)

(5)

On a road, the hunt underway. The troop is now horseless. Haggard, Bayles pulls Tituba's cart. The saddle bags are in the cart, also. Mobley rings the witching bell.

HOGG: The first field we stole on broke them horses.

BAYLES: Well, did you tell Reverend Parris before we undertook
        that a horse is no good in these fields? No, y' did not.

HOGG: Pass the oats an' shut your face. *(Bayles passes beer.)*

MOBLEY: I'm too old for this much walk.

STOUGHTON: Come, sir, I am near your age and still walk;
        A quarter hour every morning
        Is first thing on the day's docket for me.
        It will keep the abdomen down and calf
        Up firm. Think that you walk with God, is all.

MOBLEY: There is small deity in Hogg and Bayles, sir.

STOUGHTON: True, they are a wet pair, but no matter.
        Their refreshment keeps them up and sportive.

MOBLEY: Can we stop, sir?

STOUGHTON: Yes, a minute's sit would be good for all.
        A brief pause will make the quick man quicker.
        Mister Parris, where does this witch habit?

PARRIS: Well, the hovel with her sorry mate, sir,
　　　　Where we found her not, or any broad field
　　　　In God's creation, or any house
　　　　Or barn, or hay mound, under any tree,
　　　　Or anywhere a soul can get to walking.

STOUGHTON: That does cut it down fine.

PARRIS:　　　　　　　　　　　　　　Never near water.
　　　　The thing does not wash.

CALEF:　　　　　　　　　Good then, she passes by
　　　　Any body of water. That's proof
　　　　Enough of contact with the devil.

STOUGHTON: Why, my good Mister Calef, expound that.
　　　　Though I have never heard it recognized
　　　　It does sound plausible. What reference
　　　　Do you cite?

CALEF:　　　　　　Revelations, Mr. Stoughton.

PARRIS: The Lord pardon his errant minister;
　　　　I am ignorant of this passage.

STOUGHTON: What passage is it, sir, that fogs us both?

CALEF: Oh, no passage; I must beg your pardons.
　　　　It is some knowledge, revelatory
　　　　Therefore, out of Greek philosophy.
　　　　One of a number of popular sophists
　　　　Once predicated earth to be composed

Of air, water and fire, in combine,
And this triad composition was all
Of matter and all that mattered, also.
So, Mr. Stoughton, if Satan passes air
And witches water, their bold committee
Is in evidence.

STOUGHTON: Oh, Mister Calef!

PARRIS: Yes, what of the fire, though?

CALEF: C'est nous, Monsieur.

PARRIS: I am weak on language; is that Latin?

STOUGHTON: It is doggerel, Parris, profanation
Desecration, impious sacrilege,
Odium theologicum (that's Latin),
With a dash of self-mismanagement,
And I detest the presence of it here!

CALEF: I have never seen a body thus cut,
Chained, carted and magically condemned.
I have aversion to it.

STOUGHTON: What, have I
No senses? Does it not sting me, d'you think?
But do I blush and fumble, fluctuate?
I am rod and staff here, emissary
To our good Christian doctrine and God's will.
It is a relic of longevity
And sign of stern survival, this witch hunt.

No man can make it otherwise, or kind
Upon his eyes. It burns, it does impress,
But must be clinched. Calef, shall I watch a sore
On this arm grow till I submit my life
Or hack the arm at its elbow and live?
It is as simple as that. Good conscience
Is most laudatory in you but revolt
Is out. Pray you, dispel it here and now
If it does jab you. Parry, and be done.
(Calef says nothing but mimes the parry of a foil.)
There rides our Witch of Endor, believe it,
Our Saul in this is young Ann Putnam
Who did recount to me this same morning
How her mother sent her to Tituba
To have raised the seven children's spirits
Goody Putnam lost in childbirth.
Seven, mark. All lost. The seven infants
Equate to Samuel. Now tell me, Calef,
That nothing is in likeness here to scripture,
No smack, no parallel, no homologue,
Nothing.

CALEF: I cannot dispute on those terms.

STOUGHTON: Why, name your own.

CALEF: Sheer wonder does prohibit
      me a ground.

STOUGHTON: Then we shall have to proceed
      On my ground, My terms, my experience.

CALEF: Your servant, sir, till mine are better formed.

STOUGHTON: It is procession time, Mister Parris,
     The bell, sir, we will move out.
     (Bell is sounded, some move out.)

CALEF: Why the bell, sir?

STOUGHTON: It's an old English or Dane solution
     To harassment of the hunters by the witch.
     It will negate any spirit she sends.

CALEF: A kind of provident umbrella, then.
     After you, sir.

(6)

A field, Sarah Good.

SARAH: *(ENTERS)* How do I know a fir from an oak? *(She looks left, she looks right, looks rear, then front)* Fir, said 'e. *(She arches her back, supporting the small of it with both palms and recovers. She sits on a rock. She scratches her leg, somewhere beneath her yards of ankle length rags. She rolls her shoulders, scratches a blade. Sarah Good is very tired. She unhooks and takes off her shoes, throwing them disgustedly. Stands on her stockinged feet, shifts her weight, mumbling. Sits down. She concentrates blankly and haggardly on something distant, alone and forlorn. She cannot see that far, but rests her eyes, thereby letting all the senses of the mind go numb. The exquisite warble of a thrush is heard, as disconsonant a note as could be imagined with Sarah Good present. She looks up, then off, back of her, then gives it up.)* I'm hungry. *(Scratches her matted head, inspects the hand that did the scratching, drops it to her knee in disgust. She wails a terrifying, throaty, cry of resignation and recovers.)* I ain't no witch. Damn 'em for their witches. *(The thrush is heard again. She looks off, then up, back of her, gives it up, mumbles. Sarah picks an insect from her sleeve. She pulls out her pipe, impossible to light since there is no fire. She confronts the hopeless with a grunt, puts the pipe in her mouth, stands.)* It is gettin' dark. *(She retrieves her shoes, sits again, puts them on loose. She puts her hand on her belly, stares contemptuously at the ground, recovers from both together. A long song from the thrush allows her to locate his direction. Halfway through the composition, she dejectedly returns her eyes to the ground in front of her. The bird ceases. She looks in the direction of her exit, opposite her entrance, then stands.)* Oh, oh. *(Goes a few feet from her exit, she turns to the invisible songster.)* What need I of commandments, eh? *(In the far, dim distance is heard the tolling of the witch bell. She tosses her head defiantly and slowly.)*

(EXITS)

(7)

A field, near dark. Parris, Stoughton and Calef.

PARRIS: Shall we wait on the cart?
         We are getting ahead of it, sir.

STOUGHTON: Surely, Mister Parris, those men do well
         To move that vehicle at any rate.
         It would prove brute to the stoutest ox.

PARRIS: They are drinking more now. It may slow them.

STOUGHTON: No, I think it fuels them, and without them
         We would have no cart. Do let them imbibe.
         They are hard at task.

PARRIS: There's excitement now,
         A wild behavior, seeming to point to us.

STOUGHTON: I see it and they are pointing this way.
         We will wait on it then.

CALEF: It is near dark.

STOUGHTON: For which the provident Mister Parris
         Brings us torches. The thing is well thought out.

PARRIS: I thank you, sir.

CALEF: We will go on, then?

STOUGHTON: When Abraham, against his deep foreboding,
   But briskly, nearly took his Issac's life,
   Shall we condone the dark to take a witch?
   Never, sir. The job is ours to take her.
   We are God's people; the night is Lucifer's.
   We are thieving one from Lucifer's bosom
   This night.

CALEF: To steal of the Devil is thrift.

STOUGHTON: Puritan theology is thrift, man,
   The Devil is against it here.

CALEF: This year?

STOUGHTON: Why not this year like any other?
   What does the year matter?

CALEF: It is leap year
   And look at the witches.

STOUGHTON: Is it leap year?
   Well, so it is and I might wonder, too,
   What significance was buried there
   If I believed in base superstitions.

PARRIS: Mobley yelled something, fell promptly down,
   And is up and coming fast.

STOUGHTON: True, fast for him.
   Come, man. Come, Come!

(ENTER MOBLEY)

MOBLEY: We saw 'er, Judge, beyond y' here, over in that fir row.
　　　　The witch, Good. When she spied us, she went into the trees.

STOUGHTON:　　　　　　　　　Do you mean flew into?

MOBLEY: Well, I can't state how p'cisely, but she disappeared
　　　　quick enough.

STOUGHTON: Good man.

MOBLEY: It was Tituba saw her. And says there's a great frog pond
　　　　there.

STOUGHTON:　　　　　Well, not near water, Mister Parris?
　　　　We have our witch gentlemen, and in frogs.

(ENTER HOGG AND BAYLES, PULLING THE CART WITH TITUBA)

　　　　Woman, it will go well with you for this.

TITUBA: Oh, Tituba see what you want her to,
　　　　Goody Good, the witch, Jezebel and shrew.
　　　　She is at the frog pond.

PARRIS:　　　　　　　God be with us.

STOUGHTON: Mister Hogg and Mister Bayles, can you climb
　　　　That rise?

BAYLES: Yes, sir, if it's not straight up we can climb it. *(He drinks openly and passes the beer to Hogg.)*

HOGG: Mobley?

MOBLEY: No thank y', William. I'm near finished now. I doubt m'self good for much more, wet or dry.

STOUGHTON: Sir, tip with them. It will loosen those loins,
Make pliable that knotted back and shrill
Your whistle. We need such an ardent man
To direct our cartmen. Do tip, do tip.

HOGG & BAYLES: Cheers to y', Judge Stoughton.

MOBLEY: *(Drinking)* Oh, thank y', Judge.

TITUBA: Have pity on poor slave, Mister Parris.

PARRIS: Pity. What can you think of wanting now
In your place, woman?

TITUBA: A small drink of beer,
Sir, I be frightful thirsty.

MOBLEY: *(Throwing his beer at her)* There! Drink it, y' harlot. I hope it may drown y'. What right have you t' be askin' things of good men? You're throwin' the whole countryside into fear and hidin' with your witchcraft and black magic, judgin' others, goin' on with yer damn mumbo-jumbo. God will see y' hanged yet despite yer accusin' others. Had I my way, I'd as soon see y' fish hooked at the womb this minute an' dragged till yer belly ripped. Damn y' for a witch and take the beer.

CALEF: Tell me, sir.
What Christian tenet drove you to such a speech?

MOBLEY: Fatigue, sir, forgive me.

CALEF: That's understandable, but do refill
          Your tankard, my good man.

MOBLEY: *(Does so dutifully from the cart)* Why, sir, if the
          gentleman had wanted a drink, he merely had to say the
          word. Here, drink deep, sir, an' pardon m' thoughtlessness.

CALEF: *(Emptying the tankard in Mobley's face)*
                                  Pardon my need
          Of reason; I do beg your forgiveness.

MOBLEY: It's given, sir.

CALEF: And accepted, sir; now, then, replenish.

MOBLEY: *(He does with some anxiety)* Here, sir.

CALEF: *(Hands the tankard up to Tituba who takes it.)*
          Drink, woman, and I will see a medic
          Attends to that face early this evening.
          There is a careless similarity
          In Salem between the accusation,
          Judgement and due and rightful sentence
          That I detest. They all wear the same hat,

Draining method, denying innocence.
Sorcery and witchcraft are endemic
In the town, caught in the craw, and their vomit
Stinks to heaven.

STOUGHTON: You cross me again, sir.

CALEF: No, sir, I am, I hope, a gentleman
        Who wants no woman in his sight abused
        Unjustly.

STOUGHTON: To the frog pond! Move out that cart!
        Enough of this. You agreed with me once
        You came in search of rugged evidence
        Of witchcraft, and that is coming - not arrived.
        Quail not, Mister Calef. Come off your toes,
        Man, and walk with us on your foot's ball,
        Make stout your gait and firm your heart.
        Those quick feelings withhold and tongue lash tight
        And I will show you hell on earth!
        Do you still care? Will you follow?

(EXIT HOGG, BAYLES, MOBLEY, TITUBA AND CART)

CALEF: Right, lead on.

(EXIT CALEF, STOUGHTON, AND PARRIS)

(8)

The frog pond. Sarah Good. The bell is heard distantly. It is darker.

SARAH: *(Mumbles, as before.)* I ain't no witch; I know no witches. Confound yer bell. *(Wipes her brow; takes a deep breath.)* I keep no traffic with no Devil. It is me, Goodwife Good, y' fools. Not worth the chase. *(Mumbles, looks in the direction of the bell sound.)* A poor catch, hear me? I ain't no witch and know none. Damn your Tituba. Damn the children. Damn all of y'. *(She stumbles to all fours.)* Sure I might deserve that. Way of the needy. There's more no good ministers in Hell and decent sinners in Heaven than poor either place, I wager. There is nowhere for our likes but somewhere to fall. So, where is my hole? Haw. A crag for the hag. Y' dimwit. *(Mumbles, sits on the ground; for the moment she is too tired to rise. Sarah is suddenly alarmed by something in her lap. She picks up by the hind leg of a frog, holds him aloft, screams a frenzied, demoniac scream and hurls the frog from her.)* Oh, oh, what is happening to ol' Sar'? What goes here? How comes a frog in Sarah's lap? Frogs come of devils, damnation. I'm damned, I am. Sarah Good is damned. There is a whole pond of them. *(The bell is louder.)* And I am damned. A whole pond of devil frogs, and it is too dark to run more. *(She wails.)* I have been undone. I have been run into a cursed frog pond. *(Wails)*

(9)

The field. The pursuers, pressing hard. The bell busy. Frogs croaking in the distance.

HOGG: *(Stopping)* Curses, my ankle. These stones are hard on
    walking.

BAYLES: A minute here. Wilfred has twisted his ankle.

PARRIS: Need you curse, Mister Hogg?

HOGG: No need, Reverend. I beg pardon for it.

PARRIS: Is it sprained, d' you think?

HOGG: No, just turned.

PARRIS: The Devil, turning us, slowing us down.

TITUBA: And what do you think I have endured
    These hours? The irons gouge my ankles.
    The hooking of the cart has sprained them both
    To swelling and my ribs are feeling cracked
    And bruised on both my sides. You are sparrows
    For the pity shown. Wrens. No, hummingbirds.
    But let a man turn his ankle, and come
    Ministers.

PARRIS: You must be less vocal, witch.

CALEF: Charity, woman. Christian charity.

TITUBA: Sir, you jest.

CALEF: With my whole heart, I do.

STOUGHTON: Hurry there. We will be needing torches.
        Shortly. What ails you this time, sheriff Hogg?

HOGG: A good rub will fix it, sir.

STOUGHTON: Well, then, rub and get on. The light is gone.
        Moreover, I now think I heard her laugh
        Or shout. Mend, can't you?

TITUBA: Tituba hear her cry!

STOUGHTON: Come, man. We must close on her.

HOGG: Yes, sir.

STOUGHTON: Watch your ground, Gentlemen. Another slip
        Could mean sure loss of her. Move, by God, move.
        (The cart is rolling again.)

MOBLEY: I cannot cut it, Mister Stoughton, without some rest. My
        joints say no to it. *(Sits)*

STOUGHTON: *(Taking the bell, ringing it clamorously)*
        Now, by Heaven, we will take the woman
        At the height of her misconduct, spell bound.
        At Satan's charm, in eroticism,

Incantation, necromancy, black art,
All the invocation, conjuration,
That must brand them blackened witches all.
Now, make ready for the unbelievable;
Keep close with God and move to it.

(10)

The frog pond. Sarah Good. The bell louder. Frogs croaking.

SARAH: *(She has moved back from the pond, but is still seated on the ground.)* The slithery devils are everywhere, croakin' an' jumpin', bulgin' their damned eyes out. I ne'er be afraid of frogs before. Well, I'm come to it now. *(Off)* Hang yer heathen bell. It does no more point to God than a cow bell does. *(Mumbles)* Y' vultures. Y' carrion hunters. *(She inspects her skirts.)* I'm wet through. And cold. Ah, William, where can y' be, y' cannot come an' pull yer ol' baggage, Sar', out of this? Where are y' now, husband? I know, I know; it was me that left. *(She looks into the trees.)* But I could not learn them commandments. There was ten t' fix in mind. Thou shalt not steal. *(Pause)* Thou shalt not covet—something. Agh. Thou shalt not this an' that. It is full of nots. What moves up there? I saw it plain. I say, who moves? *(She squints, adjusts, to see; peers. Looks away, Looks back.)* Hanged if I did not see y'. *(She throws up a stone; in answer to which is a large flutter of wings. It causes Sarah to fall to her back in the grass.)* Oh, ministers of Grace, defend. Defend. Out, damn y' out. Sarah Good is a goodly woman. Touch me not. Lay by your hand. Oh, touch me not. Heaven will take vengeance on y'. Mind it now. *(She sits up.)* And if Heaven do not, I will m'self. Count on it. *(Feeling her back)* Soppin' wet, damn the devils hereabout. I'm soaked to the skin, top to bottom, and am cold as ice. A mess, look here. *(She brushes another frog from her shoulder.)* Ahhh! Taunted. Banned and trapped. Send no more spirits. Fright me no more. I will be yours. Sarah Good will belong to the Devil. Oh, send no more. *(Wails, wrings her hands.)* Send

no more spirits. Fright me no more. Pity, Goody Good, oh, pity on her. She'll be yours to use, but raise her up from fear, oh , raise her. Mercy, mercy, Devil. Take me and have mercy. *(The bell, having grown consistently louder, now stops)* Sarah good will be Satan's witch. There'll be no cause for more fear. Now God watch his step. New power comes to this old hag. She can dance now, make spells, bake witch's cake, send out spirits, put animals in pain, ring church bells for a look, suck ugly teats on the bodies of her children, make sticks fly, and fly herself. Sure, I do covenant with you, Devil. Take Sarah Good. Let the little frogs come into Sarah's apron, into Sarah's dress, an' , yes, into Sarah's body. *(Wails, entices
the frogs.)* Come, come, come, now. Come.

(ENTER STOUGHTON)

STOUGHTON: Seize her!

(ENTER PARRIS, WHO DOES THE SEIZING, CALEF, AND BAYLES AND HOGG PULLING TITUBA'S CART)

HOGG: *(Now helping Parris secure Sarah)* That's the wench.

STOUGHTON: Yes, this is one worth the chase, alright.
　　　We've had confession before it was asked for.

HOGG: Where is my horse?

STOUGHTON: She knows nothing of horses now, Mister Hogg.
　　　She is in a creation of her frenzy,
　　　Whipped to the shadowy fantastical.

Feeble minded in the world we know,
She is ingenious plotter in her own.
She is an unembellished thing.

BAYLES: Frogs everywhere.

STOUGHTON: There, Mister Calef, is a witch.
    You heard her invoke and allege to Satan.
    What do you think of your limpid doubts now?

CALEF: I hardly know; I am struck by it,
    I would reserve my judgement for some time.

STOUGHTON: By my word, you have heard nothing yet.
    Tituba, will you name this woman.

TITUBA: Goody Good, sir.

STOUGHTON: Which side of Purgatory
    Does she habit?

TITUBA: Only the dark side, sir.

STOUGHTON: Who commands her? Lucifer?

TITUBA: Lucifer.

STOUGHTON: Well, still doubting are you, sir? Does she keep
    Witches company? I would have some names.

TITUBA: I cannot see them. They repel the light,
　　　　Sir, breaking it off. A sea of black masks
　　　　Is all that comes to Tituba now.
　　　　I cannot tell who these companions be;
　　　　She know them by name.

STOUGHTON:　　　　　　　　　　Sarah, Sarah Good!

SARAH: Yes, yes.

STOUGHTON: You hear?

SARAH: Yes.

STOUGHTON: Are you assured of what you hear?

SARAH: What, sir?

STOUGHTON: Do you understand me, catch my meaning?

SARAH: I do.

STOUGHTON: Witches unconfessed will hang by the neck
　　　　In Salem. Acknowledge yourself. Give up
　　　　This wicked nature and restore to God.
　　　　Speak, woman, and divulge your black secrets.

SARAH: I'm cold, sir, cold.

STOUGHTON: And will get colder lest I hear confession
　　　　From you. For when the neck snaps and heart stops,
　　　　A tomblike cold invades the whole body.

So, would you hang a damned witch, or confess
Your company?

SARAH: Who, who? What company?

STOUGHTON: On my soul, I hear an owl;
          I took you for an old bat. I begin
          Over. Witches do not singly travel,
          But in flocks. Name me your confederates.

SARAH: I'm a lone hag in it, all alone.

PARRIS: That is a lie; Tituba has seen them,
          Your partisan and fellow crones. We've proof!

SARAH: Tituba? Then let her name. She know me, she know Goody
          Osburne. She know 'em all.

STOUGHTON: That woman has seen the angelic light.
          Though she will go to prison for sorcery,
          She will not hang for witchcraft. Choose your road,
          Woman.

SARAH: I am alone, I tell y'.

STOUGHTON: One of you lies. Nor shall anyone
          Bear false witness, or liquefy his tongue,
          But speak straightforward and in breach
          Of no commandment. Now, wheresoever
          It will fall from, let it come, and be truth.
          For in truth is your salvation. *(Silence)*

CALEF: I protest.

STOUGHTON: You may do that, but in court, sir, in time.

CALEF: You have set them against one another
           Like two elk proportionately antlered
           And similarly dumb. It is a test
           Of will.

STOUGHTON: How discerning, Mister Calef.
           You do learn something here despite protest.

CALEF: They are both of them in need of lawyers.

PARRIS: There are none in Salem, Mister, or welcome.
           They are not countenanced here.

CALEF: ·   I beg you,
          Judge Stoughton.

STOUGHTON: Speak, one of you and with care.

SARAH: What do I care for yer commandments? Y' would hang me for a
          witch if I do not name. I give y' names. Rebecca Nurse is a witch,
          an' Elizabeth Proctor, an'—

PARRIS: Rebecca Nurse!

STOUGHTON: Her!

BAYLES: Elizabeth Proctor.
          That cannot be of such a Christian woman.

SARAH: Sure, an' her husband, John Proctor. An' that's not all, there—

HOGG: John Proctor cannot be.

PARRIS: Upon my Christian oath, of Rebecca
     That sainted soul, I never could have thought—
     Let linger, even—

STOUGHTON: Chain the wench to the cart
     And leave us go—

SARAH: There's—

STOUGHTON: Desist, by Heaven. You bleed
     Some stout names, and warrants will be issued
     For them. But I warn you consider hard,
     Prior to more naming, that you saw them
     In your conjurations, not in mere dreams,
     Or in wrath, or envy, jealousy—

SARAH: Witches, all!

STOOUGHTON: Let us move out then, establish here a court,
     And see how far this thing will take us.
     We are uncovering a pack when things
     Looked timid.

SARAH: Witches, all!

STOUGHTON: Calef, I read amazement,
     Discernment toppled with judgement vexed.
     Do you learn something new here?

CALEF: *(Preoccupied)*   What, sir?

STOUGHTON: I say have you learned something new?

CALEF: I have seen something new that old learning
       Has quite forgot, and must be relearned
       Every so many years as would make fools
       Of imbeciles, heretics of madmen,
       Conquerors of belly scratchers
       Or with best of fortune, men of mad dogs.
       It has novelty, but nothing new, sir.

(EXIT ALL)

(11)

The Salem Meeting House arranged as a court. Five girls sit to one side as though in a jury box, Abigail, Betty, young Ann Putnam, and two others. Abigail is their spokesman. Reverend Parris is below and to one side of Stoughton, as court recorder. Calef and a small party sit opposite the girls.

STOUGHTON: Sheriff Hogg, have you retrieved your horse, sir?

HOGG: I found 'er this morning, sir, thank you.
STOUGHTON: Then we will not charge Sarah Good with payment
      For it. But I would determine now
      That all accused that are condemned in this court
      Forfeit property and holdings to it
      In accord with law. Further, I am informed
      That both in Andover and in Boston
      Witches are discovered, accused and tried.
      This bodes well, that in our Christian land
      Sin goes not without its recognition
      And most prompt defeat. It strongly signals
      A just intolerance with Satan
      And the will to have him crushed among us.
      So, let us proceed. Bring the prisoner,
      Tituba.

(ENTER TITUBA IN IRONS, ATTENDED.)

      Now, Tituba of Barbados,
      How do you plead to sorcery?

TITUBA: Guilty, sir.

STOUGHTON: Have you cast spells, conjured and afflicted
These dear and innocent children?

TITUBA: Yes, sir.

STOUGHTON: Did you, on request of Goody Sibley
In this court, compound and bake a witch cake?
Was the cake of rye meal, children's urine,
Then fed to the Reverend Parris' dog?

TITUBA: Yes.

STOUGHTON: Did you teach these children dancing?

TITUBA: I did.

STOUGHTON: And confess all?

TITUBA: Yes, all.

STOUGHTON: You saw others?

TITUBA: I saw Goody Good and Goody Osburne.

STOUGHTON: Return the woman to her cell, and send
The prisoner Osburne.

(EXIT TITUBA, ATTENDED. ENTER SARAH OSBURNE, ATTENDED)

STOUGHTON: Sarah Osburne.

OSBURNE: Yes, sir.

STOUGHTON: Do answer, please, on the question,
     No other time. The little protocol
     This court must call for does require
     Following. You stand accused of witchcraft;
     How do you plead?

OSBURNE: Why, I plead innocent.

STOUGHTON: That is to be obstinate, and flirt with death.

OSBURNE: I would sooner seek death than the Devil.

STOUGHTON: Why, woman, to die a witch is to travel
     With Satan hereafter. Repent yourself
     And live with God.

OSBURNE: I'm not a witch. I never flew
     Or frightened so much as my own cat, sir.

STOUGHTON: Nor these children?

OSBURNE: No, sir.

STOUGHTON: What do they say?

ABIGAIL: She has poppets.

OSBURNE: Them are old, Abigail, and mere shadows
     Of my childhood, stored in trunks, forgotten.

STOUGHTON: They are forbidden.

OSBURNE: So, it seems, is love.

STOUGHTON: You are not here to accuse this court
        But to defend yourself, Sarah Osburne.
        How will you plead?

OSBURNE: Before you I'm guilty.
        Before these children, I'm held also guilty.
        But before my God I am innocent.
        I will keep peace there in preference
        To the court, if it please you.

STOUGHTON: It does not,
        And you are sentenced to hang by the neck
        Till dead come Tuesday next. Bring Sarah Good.

(EXIT SARAH OSBURNE, ATTENDED. ENTER SARAH GOOD, WELL ATTENDED.)

        (To Calef who has stood up)
        Whyever do you stand, Mr. Calef?

CALEF: I do beg the pardon of the court sir,
        An unwarranted reaction, too quick. *(Reseats)*

STOUGHTON: By my God, do you never wash, woman?

GOOD: There is not enough water in Salem to wash me.

STOUGHTON: How do you plead in this court to witchcraft?
        It gives you opportunity to cleanse,
        In a fashion.

GOOD: I would stay dirty.

STOUGHTON: What meaning is in that?

GOOD: And confess.

STOUGHTON: You plead guilty, then?

GOOD: Can I confess that I am innocent?

STOUGHTON: Yes, and in sainthood, too.

GOOD: Haw!

STOUGHTON: How do you plead?

GOOD: As I must, guilty.

STOUGHTON: I waive your deposition, as is right,
        That John and Goodwife Proctor are witches,
        Too. So, too, of Goody Nurse. Are these true
        Accusations?

GOOD: Aye, my life on it, so to speak.

STOUGHTON: What do you mean, "so to speak"?

GOOD: Then, plain and simple.

STOUGHTON: I like that no better, plain and simple.

GOOD: Well, sir, take yer pick 'tween the two; they're all from me.

STOUGHTON: Why, that is contempt and will be charged you.
   Enter it, Mister Parris, and guard take her.
   Bring me these Proctors.

(EXIT SARAH UNDER GUARD AND ENTER JOHN AND ELIZA-BETH PROCTOR, GUARDED)

ABIGAIL: *(Screams)* It is the frog from my uncle's pasture. It is
   catching insects! It croaks and it croaks. I cannot hear my
   God! Frogs are everywhere! Oh, Heaven hear me!

GIRLS: Oh, Heaven hear me.

ABIGAIL: I am bleeding.

(EXIT ABIGAIL RUNNING)

STOUGHTON: Send a matron to her.
   Have her attended and return soon.
   Proctors, what do you bring here? Enchantment,
   Magic, sorcery? This is reckless damage
   To reveal in a court. What do you mean?

PROCTOR: We do not cause the girl's affliction, sir.
   We both fear God as Christians and know
   His commandments. There is no truth in charges
   Made against our good names, no truth in much
   Of this. The Devil is at work here, surely.

STOUGHTON: Something apparent you have voiced at last,
   Mister Proctor. The Devil works here.
   What do you think of his labors so far?

PROCTOR: Why, marvelous, sir, most marvelous.

STOUGHTON: An apt description; the disciple's muse
       Comes, warming your head with liquored summary
       Of it. Why is it marvelous?

ELIZABETH: It is to be marveled at, sir, was meant.

PROCTOR: The girls have all entered womanhood, sir.
       All are the age, every one.

STOUGHTON: No sir, you err.
       Some, not here, are older and can recognize
       Their natural signs.

PROCTOR: It is manifest
       Hysteria, sir, and can be whipped out.

STOUGHTON: Ah, then do it, John Proctor, here's a switch.
       Convert them. *(Proctor takes the switch.)*

PROCTOR: Surely you know, I cannot
       Step toward them or they will climb the walls.

STOUGHTON: I suspect so.

BETTY: Abigail!

(EXIT BETTY RUNNING)

ANN: I will not stay here.

(EXIT ANN PUTNAM)

STOUGHTON: What do you send at them?

PARRIS: Yes, what form, man?

(THE REMAINING TWO GIRLS CRY OUT AND LEAVE RUNNING)

PROCTOR: *(Amazed)* It is quite marvelous,

STOUGHTON: To see your work well done? It's marvelous?
    A marvel is some work of sorcery,
    Masked and cloaked in its underworldly dress,
    Denying any natural aspect
    And happening before our seeing eyes
    But, as to meaning, it will signify
    Not what we note, but something absent.
    I do charge you, sir, with the emptying,
    Therefore, all of those persons in this court,
    By demonology, who could and would
    Convict the two of you in witchcraft.
    It was a clever scheme, but will reverse
    When they are promptly brought in. *(To a Guard)* Guard, see
    To it.

(EXIT GUARD)

ELIZABETH: John, I'm afraid they will have us hanged.

STOUGHTON: Goody Proctor, when you were served your warrant
    Was there found a poppet in your house
    Pierced with needles?

ELIZABETH: Mary Warren put it there.

STOUGHTON: True, she both confesses and denies it
          And so we will discount her testimony.
          Was it there or not there?
ELIZABETH: Yes, it was there.

(ENTER GUARD)

GUARD: Sir, the girl, Abigail, is in a fit. Wriggling in pain and
          dizzy, she says, and all blood. She refuses to return 'til the
          Proctors are gone. And the other girls swear to stay by her.
          None will come.

STOUGHTON: The evidence is damning. Go you two
          To jail and there confess or hang come Tuesday.
          I'll have no more of this in my own court
          Or elsewhere, anymore. Witches will hang
          Like crows in corn fields gather, before they break
          This good community. Go, witches both.

ELIZABETH: It's done, John.

PROCTOR: It is so, Elizabeth,
          And God's will likely. But how is it done?
          I say how?

*(EXIT THE PROCTORS ATTENDED AND REBECCA NURSE IS
BROUGHT IN)*

STOUGHTON: Rebecca Nurse, is it?

PARRIS: Yes, Judge Stoughton, she has been in her bed
 Ill these last eight or nine days. She is weak
 And old, sir. Sit down, Rebecca, sit.

STOUGHTON: The accusations against her are heavy.
 They have grown since Sarah Good's confession
 Like wind gathers wind. I have recorded
 That a Goodman Kenny was afflicted
 By a visit from her. One Edward Putnam,
 Saw her trance his niece and Goody Putnam,
 Our younger Ann's mother, will lay murder
 At her door. The woman, Nurse, has midwifed
 Seven babes of Putnam and all died. All.
 How do you answer these, Goody Nurse?

(ENTER THE CHILDREN, TAKING THEIR PLACES. ABIGAIL HAS
ON AN OVERSKIRT)

NURSE: I never hurt no child, never.

STOUGHTON: Nor, by God, afflicted Goodman Kenny?

NURSE: No, nor no one.

STOUGHTON: You say no to all accounts against you.

NURSE: I am in God's way, ever and ever.

STOUGHTON: Then, I ask you, why do these children agree
 With the witch Good that you have power.

NURSE: I know not.

STOUGHTON: Tell me, who does have power over you?

NURSE: God has it all.

STOUGHTON: She has the glassy stare of one half dead
        But I find no uncivility in her.

PARRIS: And, sir, she has a following of good friends
        And excellent family. She is a rock
        Of Puritan faith and is regular
        In Church.

NURSE: As God is my witness.

STOUGHTON: I cannot fathom it, then.

(ENTER MISTER HOGG)

HOGG: Judge Stoughton, I have a deposition from a score of
        friends who will stand by Rebecca Nurse's character.

STOUGHTON: Let me see. It preaches flawless character
        And comes heavily signed. Mister Parris,
        Are those worthy signatures?

PARRIS: The best, sir.

STOUGHTON: Yet seven children dead in infancy.

NURSE: Some stillborn. The mother was weak.

STOUGHTON: There is no more here; I will pass on it.

NURSE: God praise you, sir.

STOUGHTON: The accusations will not bear up;
        The children do now appear unafflicted.
        Rebecca Nurse is innocent as charged
        And free to go.

ABIGAIL: *(Screams)* No!

GIRLS: No!

ABIGAIL: She is guilty!

GIRLS: She is guilty!

ABIGAIL: Look there the frog.

GIRLS: The crippled dog!

ABIGAIL: All does portend!

GIRLS: She does pretend!

ALL: We have seen Rebecca fly,
        Seen her bake a witch's pie.
        Guilty, guilty!
        We have seen Rebecca die
        Without a grave to occupy.

        She would work on Sabbath Day,
        Lead our working men astray.
        Guilty, guilty!

She will live on caraway
Stolen from the popinjay.
She is fraudulent and old,
Lies come from her thousand-fold.
Guilty, guilty!
She has crushed our marigold,
Brought Satan to her household!
We have seen Rebecca die
Without a grave to occupy!

GIRLS: The crippled dog!

ABIGAIL: Look at the frog!

ALL: She sends them out
      And calls us liar;
      Be that devout?
      The door's ajar!

STOUGHTON: Slam shut that door! (The door is slammed)
      There, now.

PARRIS: It does portend—

GIRLS: She does pretend. *(The girls quail and group together.)*

STOUGHTON: Answer to it.

NURSE: Lies, lies!

ALL: *(Mimicking)* Lies, lies.

NURSE: Yes, untruth.

ALL: Yes, untruth.

PARRIS: Why, she has them.

STOUGHTON: Every one.

NURSE: Angels of mercy.

ALL: Angels of mercy.

STOUGHTON: In her palm.

NURSE: Little harlots all.

ALL: Little harlots all.

STOUGHTON: Enough! Next Tuesday, are you not confessed
          Of witchcraft, you will hang by the neck
          Till dead for this and other perpetrations
          Of it. Let loose these children and go think
          Upon it. I say let them loose. Go, go
          And may God restore your allegiances.
          Now go. Take your deceptions with you
          And leave this court. A shame upon such actions
          In God's view and under obligation
          To these, his unoffending servants.
          Go, now.

(EXIT REBECCA NURSE, ESCORTED.)

Thus withdraw deception, craft and cunning
Rare among us, unregistered misconduct,
Artful depravity and outrage veiled.
Goodness has all within it, would we search.
So must this court resent beguilement,
Follow truth and, like the purposed hunter,
Bring home that thing we most do crave.
(Calef stands)
Mister Calef?

CALEF: Observing our friendship, sir,
And my own high respect for your purpose
Here, I have a question of this court.

STOUGHTON: Yes.

CALEF: What evidence, sir?

STOUGHTON: I don't follow, sir.

CALEF: What convicts these people of their witchcraft?

STOUGHTON: Why, you saw it. The children do cry out.

CALEF: They see things.

STOUGHTON: Yes, they do!

CALEF: Which no one else sees.

STOUGHTON: True, true!

CALEF: Because they are afflicted.

STOUGHTON: Here, do make your point, please, Mister Calef.

CALEF: Why, my point is that brilliant coxcomb
      On the Reverend Parris' head.

STOUGHTON: That's irreverent.
      What in Heaven do you mean, Mister Calef?

CALEF: It cannot be; I see it plain as light.
      I see it bright red and halfway parted;
      Some goes this way, some that. It's some rooster's
      And will be missed.

STOUGHTON: Even by our friendship
      I will not now allow such tasteless humor
      On these premises. I gave you good time
      For serious questioning.

CALEF: So I do use
      And not abuse it, sir. My word on it.

STOUGHTON: Are you possessed, man? There is nothing there.

CALEF: I say only that your court recorder
      Is part cock, no more.

STOUGHTON: Mister Calef, sir!

CALEF: I am possessed, therefore.

Robert Manns

STOUGHTON: You must be,
    Or will stand in contempt of this court!

CALEF: Then I am not possessed. If I am charged,
    That precedent will bring five girls to trial,
    As well. Do charge me, I beg you, Stoughton.

STOUGHTON: Why, why, do you wish the girls charged, Calef?

CALEF: No, sir, it is who, who, that makes an owl
    Of an old bat. Do you remember her?
    I must herewith cry this court a fraud
    And, marked by superstition as it is,
    Impossible of justice. Its evidence
    Unreal, imaginary, lied to,
    Tends more to social spite and haggery
    Than fact. It's pure religious heresy,
    Concoction and device, and I am done
    With it.

STOUGHTON: Then you are done with me, also.

CALEF: No, sir, not quite yet am I done with you
    Till I have seen our Governor in Boston.
    The girls are frosted liars. Evidence
    They cannot be, or that taken for, here
    Or nowhere. This I intend with promptness
    To see to.

STOUGHTON: And respect for my purpose here,
    As you put it?

CALEF: Did I put it so, sir?
          It's prosecution in a wild passion,
          Too divest of knowledge, some compassion,
          A grain of feeling even or inroad
          Toward clemency. My God, it's Attila
          With a rope!

PARRIS: I never liked you from the start!

CALEF: My regrets, sir, and apologies.
          You have no coxcomb but are made an asshead
          By belief, just as we all are prone.
          I do thank the court.

(EXIT CALEF)

STOUGHTON: The court is adjourned
          Till morning of the morrow.

(12)

Salem Meeting House, the following morning. All are present but Mr. Calef.

(ENTER STOUGHTON)

STOUGHTON: Hear the court.
    In our enraptured time on truth's behalf,
    Fully assembled but only half conscious
    Of some ultimate or final meaning,
    This devout court and all its assemblage
    Has overlooked too captivated long
    That where there goes mob there, too, goes leadership.
    So, as our blind search grew dim and promised light
    The name then arose of black minister.
    Not sudden did it, for the girls, Tituba
    And witch Hobbs had decried him weeks hence.
    He was virile, pleasant to look on,
    Powerful, and, most lamentable to us,
    A learned and flocked minister.
    Small Ann Putnam was first namer of him.
    Thereupon, his misdeeds grew in number
    And the girl did letter them in detail.
    Now has his spectered shape choked her to silence.
    The man, once holder of a parish here,
    Was forcibly procured last night from Boston,
    And will stand trial for crime he denies.
    So look with small fascination now,
    For if he is convicted guilty
    As charged it will be as mentor and lode
    To all our witches, Satan's emissary.
    Bring in the Reverend Burroughs.

(ENTER BURROUGHS UNDER GUARD. HE DOES NOT, AS INSTRUCTED, LOOK AT THE GIRLS, BUT FORCIBLY AVOIDS THEM)

STOUGHTON: Sir, I will address you Mister in the court
    Since I hardly know who you serve in truth.
    How do you plead?

BURROUGHS: Innocent, by my God.

STOUGHTON: What loss will you incur if convicted?

BURROUGHS: No loss, sir, I am poor and cannot fill
    John Putnam's coffer.

STOUGHTON: What of John Putnam?

BURROUGHS: My accuser's father, a shrewd merchant,
    Did accuse me once of breach of payment,
    Brought me to court and had proved to him
    To his mild discredit, that I had paid
    The debt. He has fed my name, I trust,
    Into his daughter's mind, that court being
    Judge and jury, sure conviction, all in one.

STOUGHTON: You mistake, Mister, I am judge here.

BURROUGHS: So am I minister, yet am I lost
    To recognition.

STOUGHTON: You have a wily tongue,
    Mister, too quick, too wise. You say innocent
    To your charges.

BURROUGHS: Correct.

STOUGHTON: Let him be searched.
          For excrescence.
          (Burroughs is stripped to the waist and examined)

BURROUGHS: Why, I am a man of God,
          A minister ordained.

STOUGHTON: Nothing to fear.
          (To Bayles, who does the examining)
          Be particular with the scalp for wens.

BURROUGHS: Oh, yes, and top thoughts occasionally.

BAYLES: Nothing, sir, I have looked 'im over carefully; he is well built.

STOUGHTON: Now, Mr. Bayles, look at the girl's arms
          And report your findings to the court.

BAYLES: *(He does so)* Why, they all, every one, have marks on 'em.
          Toothbitten they are.

STOUGHTON: Did you bite them, Mister Burroughs?

BURROUGHS: I did not!

STOUGHTON: Turn and look here at your accuser now!
          (Burroughs does, for the first time. Ann Putnam screams)

ANN: The black minister!

ALL: The Devil, praise God, the Devil, praise God, the Devil, praise
   God, the Devil, praise God, *(One girl wails high and clear in the
   background)* the Devil, praise God, the Devil, praise God, the
   Devil, praise God. *(Total silence)* The black minister. *(Total
   silence. The girls suddenly begin ensemble jumping, crying
   "Oh", covering their arms as though being bitten.)*

(ENTER HOGG, DURING THE ABOVE, CONFIDES SOMETHING
TO STOUGHTON AND EXITS)

STOUGHTON: Enough and be done. It is confirmation
   From below that hangs on you, Mister Burroughs.
   Out of the mouth of one of your own witches,
   Submitting to the smallest pressure,
   Are you damned and condemned from our prison
   And to it, till high hanging time.

BURROUGHS: Pressure?

STOUGHTON: Your capture was a blessing; take him.

BURROUGHS: Torture?

STOUGHTON: What word is that, torture? What you have marked
   Upon the girls? Be done with you. Confess
   Or hang. Hang!

(EXIT BURROUGHS ATTENDED)

   (To the girls) Abigail, what may we do
   To alleviate your suffering?
   Would the girls want rest or some preference

Of a kind we would most gladly see to?
Does anything want brought in or sent for?
Would you ask a recess? There is good concern
Everywhere in Salem Towne and Village
Yes, in Andover and Beverely, too,
And Boston, for your state of health.

ABIGAIL: Nothing is needed, sir. We thank you, and I've recovered
myself.

(ENTER CALEF SITTING WHERE HE SAT IN THE PRECEDING SCENE)

STOUGHTON: *(Seeing Calef)*
Oh, no, there is misery too plenty
To accommodate more, Mister Calef.
Please remove, sir, from this poor building
And her grounds, and do it promptly
Or you will invoke my straining rage.

ALL: *(The girls become dizzy, swoon, imitate epilepsy, scream and carry on in wild convincing fashion)*
Mister Calef is a witch
Who is immune 'cause he is rich.

STOUGHTON: *(In disbelief, standing)* No!

ALL: Yes.

STOUGHTON: I say no.

ALL: We say yes.

STOUGHTON: I myself know the man.

ALL: He is no Puritan.

STOUGHTON: Why he is member, in my own parish,
       Of my congregation and does attend
       With regularity, hound-like fidelity.

ABIGAIL: Mister Calef is agnostic, sir.

CALEF: True, the girl has committed perjury
       And told the truth.

STOUGHTON: *(Sitting)* Come to the bench, sir.
       (Calef does so)
       Do you know the weight of this charge against you?
       It is heavier than agnosticism,
       Heavier than hated atheism.
       It will beget a clumsy lethargy
       And languid apathy in your mind,
       Defending itself against gloom and despair.
       It's gravity enough to bury you,
       I promise. Look now, deny the witchcraft.

CALEF: Be advised, I do.

ABIGAIL: It is a lie, I have seen you fly, Mister Calef.

CALEF: Mercy me, fly, now.

ABIGAIL: And had you pinch me.

CALEF: Deliriums of grandeur, girl. I might swat,
       But would never pinch. Too young, far too young.
       A hand on your backside would be worth ten
       Elsewhere, and calm your unsavory dreams
       For a fortnight.

STOUGHTON: Do be counseled, Calef,
       That respect—!

PARRIS: I must believe Abigail,
       She has found out another.

ABIGAIL: You put your arms around me.

PARRIS: God have mercy.

STOUGHTON: You have walked straight in, stout and foolish.

ABIGAIL: And you kissed me. *(Horrifies all but Calef)*

CALEF: Ah, then, sweet thirteen—or so. Less or more?

PARRIS: That is close enough for a guess, I think.

CALEF: Pity, it's woeful, but I am commissioned
       By our Governor Phips to deliver
       This edict to you sir, *(To Stoughton)* and hear it read
       In this court. As robin will harbinger spring
       And the jay morning, it designs to sow
       Both cordial and a buoyant atmosphere,
       In short, to drive things out of doors.

STOUGHTON: *(Reads)* How so? How so? Ah, it's done, then.
       Well you have worked it, sir, but too late.
       It throws out all evidence we use here,
       Does stamp out spectral proof in our labors
       Hence, but nowhere states reprieve for them
       So convicted.

CALEF: It was a point with him
       Not to upset the court, merely to close it.
       I will have to pursue the reprieves.

STOUGHTON: That
       Should take some time.

CALEF: Why, stay the sentences.

STOUGHTON: I cannot do that, nor let you free
       To pursue your ends. You are accused here
       And prior to this edict, sir.

CALEF: Stoughton!

STOUGHTON: It will grieve me but the presentation
       Of this paper followed accusation.

CALEF: So?

STOUGHTON: My dear sir, you came here disbelieving,
       And rode from Boston with me, by my side,
       Then joked about the very nature
       Of the Devil, jested next at witchcraft
       Itself, have called this court intolerant

Fraud, unreal, and marked by superstition,
Its evidence imaginary,
Called the girls liars and myself Attila.
I am prosecution in a passion,
Sir, to hear proclaimed we are assheads all
For our belief! It does vex me
And angers this community!
Now do I hear about agnosticism!
What are you?! Profess it cleanly!

CALEF: A man who has his private God, and, too,
A man who so beloves his wife, sir,
That he will go to church with her come Sunday,
Locked within him doubt, disfiguration,
Qualities she has not to this day used
To measure him. A man who so worships life
And living it, sups at scholarship's table,
Digesting what is usable, spurning
The rest, that he might invoke no passion
Against his neighbor's life or livelihood
For reason politic, personal
Or canonical, no passion worth murder
Being entertained. That am I,
For good or ill, profess it openly
And would not change for the world—except to save
My life.

STOUGHTON: Well, then, your life guarantees nothing.

CALEF: Nothing; it's a peaceful arrangement.

STOUGHTON: How do you swear by God, doubting him, then?

CALEF: Why, by God, by truth, by my life are all one.

STOUGHTON: It is marvelous, this notion.

PARRIS: And marvel
        Marks the Devil.

CALEF: I give life priority.
        Truth alters and is fickle. Life is composed
        Or decomposed. It will never fool, sir.

STOUGHTON: Come, come, Calef, how do you plead the charge
        Of witchcraft? I do not see how this court
        Can take your confession. It's immanent
        By your own words. It's immanent, also,
        As I see it, that the rope must have you.
        Your tongue is forked. What do you say?

CALEF: What do
        I say?

STOUGHTON: How do you plead?

CALEF: You mean to have me.

STOUGHTON: Sir I have got you. You have got yourself
        Is more charitable. I will stand
        By my convictions, give my life to them.
        The rift is now clear between us.

CALEF: A chasm.

STOUGHTON: Must we have trial to convict or will you plead,
     Mister Calef?

CALEF: Who accuses?

ABIGAIL: I do.

STOUGHTON: None else?
     There, now you have it, by Abigail.

CALEF: I make no plea and do accuse the girl,
     Abigail, of one thousand pounds worth
     Of defamation to my character
     Which she will need defend without her spells,
     Her magic and imagination,
     Since spectral evidence is barred.
     Question her, I will accept retraction. *(Total silence)*

PARRIS: Abigail, Abigail, that is a vast sum.
     Are you sure you saw him beyond all doubt?

STOUGHTON: It does not matter. Our court is shorn
     Of that evidence and must proceed now
     On material things. She is at bay!

PARRIS: *(To Calef)*
     Woe, you ever came to Salem Village.
     I cannot produce that large amount.

STOUGHTON: Guard now, girl, retract. We are overcome
     And must hope we broke the Devil here
     Before we saw this day. Recant it all.

The room is stripped of Christianity
By a pagan, once of my congregation.

CALEF: A flock grown poorer for the growing, then.

ABIGAIL: I cannot take it back.

STOUGHTON: I do not know how you can, myself,
But you must, or pay a thousand pounds.

ABIGAIL: I have no thousand pounds.

CALEF: Ability outrun by vision,
A sizable sign of youth, Abigail
And inexperience.

STOUGHTON: So, do it, now.

PARRIS: Find the strength, Abigail; I cannot find
that thousand pounds.

ABIGAIL: It is not becoming of the court, Uncle, to censure me. I speak
for God and for the good of Salem. I feel punished and dislike
it. The man mocks me, fills his pride at my expense, acts the
dandy.
His fine clothes, his neat barbered face, are false. His trousers
and his coat are cut from vanity. I think the shine on his boots
is meant to mirror his conceit when he looks down, which
must be frequent. He is a long way from God in his behavior,
hear me. Now, is all this true and me false? Do we favor
dandies? How do I gainsay what is correct? That's a new set of
rules we girls know nothing of. Must I truly lie?

PARRIS: Or lie truly, but do it.

ABIGAIL: Then in obedience no more to God but some necessity I do not understand—by your request—

PARRIS: A fine, obedient, and tortured child.

ABIGAIL: I never saw him fly, then.

CALEF: Or pinch? Never felt a pinch?

ABIGAIL: No.

CALEF: No to what, pray?

ABIGAIL: You never pinched me.

CALEF: Had I my arms around you?

ABIGAIL: No.

CALEF: No, to what?

STOUGHTON: Enough!

CALEF: No, sir, not yet. I will be cleared
          Or prosecute. To be cleared is clear of all,
          And unequivocally. Abigail?

ABIGAIL: You never put your arms around me.

CALEF: Proceed.

ABIGAIL: You never kissed me.

CALEF:　　　　　Go on.

ABIGAIL: To what, go on?

CALEF:　　　　　　　　　　The others, to Goody Nurse.

STOUGHTON: That will do sharply!

CALEF: But she is limber. I beg you, I have
　　　　Got her in the mood. Yes, in the best mood.

STOUGHTON: And you would get the most for your money.

CALEF: True, I would.

STOUGHTON:　　　　　　　Are you satisfied now?

CALEF: As with the sun when it goes down, I am
　　　　Satisfied it will come again, Stoughton.

STOUGHTON: You cannot save the others, Calef,
　　　　They are heterodoxy cast and mold.

CALEF: If the girl spurns truth hereafter,
　　　　Fiction will invade her brain, I warrant,
　　　　Onslaught after onset, outbreak and sally,
　　　　Foray, storm and certain destruction.
　　　　For the mind will bend one way and not two
　　　　Together. She may be past her honing time
　　　　This minute. Attend to her. She is a child,

Redeemable, salvageable, corrupt
But not unsuitable to love, counsel
And affection. I beg you, tend her.
Of those goodly persons now convicted,
Mind you, I do caution application
Of their sentences. Give them short stay, sir.
Permit me time to seek jurisprudence
Of some greater latitude, of some depth,
For we are all angry here, speaking quick thoughts
And old recipes.

STOUGHTON: Words will make no right
Here, Mister Calef; action shall, no else.

CALEF: Time!

STOUGHTON: It's denied.

CALEF: Stoughton! I must have time!

STOUGHTON: This court is closed, sir, by official edict.

CALEF: I must have time, Stoughton!

STOUGHTON: The court is closed.
You did hear that, did you? As for time,
That's found on any sundial.

ACT TWO

(1)

Governor Phips' house in Boston. It is Sunday morning and the large bells of a nearby church beckon the congregation to worship. A knock at the door, attended by Mary, admits Calef.

MARY: Good mornin', Mister Calef.

CALEF: Good morning , Mary. Mr. Phips is in?

MARY: The Governor is makin' ready to go to church, sir.

CALEF: So are you all; yet how many get there,
       In truth, and how many never do
       Is high mathematics. Then once arrived,
       What visions you see. It is amazing.

MARY: That is odd talk, sir.

CALEF: It's a good lesson in conformity
       To talk odd in odd times; fashionable,
       I am, then.

MARY: Why, you have always been a fashionable man, Mr. Calef.
     And a good man, and a true man and—

CALEF: Mary, can you save lives?

MARY: Me? No, sir, cannot take one, cannot save one.

CALEF: Then I would see the Governor, he can
     And must.

MARY: But I tell you, sir, he is dressin' for church.

CALEF: I have a sermon for him; go now.

MARY: I will, sir.

(EXIT MARY. CALEF EXPLORES THE ROOM, FINDS A BIBLE ON A TABLE, THUMBS THROUGH IT—LETTING HIS MOOD GROW—AND THROWS IT HARD INTO THE FIREPLACE. WHEN DONE, HE REALIZES IT IS THE GOVERNOR'S PROPERTY, AND LEAVES A POUND NOTE ON THE TABLE. ENTER MARY.)

MARY: He is bound for church, sir.

CALEF: Poor fellow! It's not the church that binds, then,
     But our need of it. I had it otherwise.
     Do untie him. I will wait, my promise.

MARY: Oh, sir, I wish you would not.

CALEF: Would not what, I ask you, wait or promise?

MARY: Either one. He is some irritable at the time. He is late, sir.

CALEF: Yes, my conceit bugs me. I know the feeling.
　　　　Some will be late to their own hangings, even.
　　　　Tell him I cannot let him go to his church,
　　　　In God's name. That should bring him out.

MARY: You are brave, Mr. Calef, is all I can say.

CALEF: Then, hope it will be enough, too. Go, please.

(EXIT MARY. CALEF SITS REVIEWING THE BIBLE IN THE FIRE-PLACE INCIDENT. CONSIDERS LONG BEFORE HE GETS UP AND ADDS ANOTHER POUND NOTE TO THE TABLE. ENTER MARY)

MARY: He was stern, sir.

CALEF: So am I, stern first. *(Sits)*

MARY: It will do no good, I fear.

CALEF: 　　　　　　　　　　Do no good, you fear?
　　　　Then John Alden and yourself, from Boston,
　　　　Accused witches both, prepare for hanging.

MARY: Am I named?

CALEF: Louder than that bell that beckons you now.

(EXIT MARY QUICKLY. JUST AS QUICKLY, CALEF MOVES TO THE TABLE, RETRIEVES ONE OF THE POUND NOTES EXCLAIMING, "It

*cannot be that much." RETURNS TO HIS SEAT, ENTER GOVERNOR
PHIPS AND MARY)*

PHIPS: I am ever pleased to see you, Calef,
            But I am off to church now, and no fool
            For it. Have they named my maid, do you say?

CALEF: I do, and John Alden.

PHIPS: Oh, John Alden, too!
            Of Mister Alden I know, but my maid!
            Spectral evidence is gone; they have no case.

CALEF: If they frighten her into confession,
            They will quickly hang her by the new rules.

PHIPS: Ah, so they have got around that, have they?
            She is a faithful servant and too valued.
            It cannot be. What do you say to it,
            Mary? Mary? You've drifted.

MARY: No, by the Lord, no, sir!

PHIPS: There, you see?
            Mistakes are made in Hell, Rarely above.
            Keep yourself indoors, Mary, 'til storm is past;
            That answers it. My breakfast.

MARY: Yes, sir, coming.

(EXIT MARY)

CALEF: You know Alden?

PHIPS: Born well, bred well, a model citizen
        Who is no more witch than—than you are, sir.
        I arranged his escape, and would yours, also.

CALEF: No need, thank you. I defended legally,
        Then censured my accuser in the court.

PHIPS: You charged? The foisty scamps. What did you do?

CALEF: No plea; and charged the girl Abigail
        With defamation, a thousand pounds worth.

PHIPS: Neat, Calef, neat. I daresay you used your head.
        That should break it; the others will follow suit.

CALEF: No, sir, there are no lawyers to advise them.

PHIPS: How many are convicted?

CALEF: None, in truth,
        But almost seventeen hanged over traps.

PHIPS: Stoughton said seven. That is a far cry
        From your number.

CALEF: He's a quick man who counts
        The season with his fingers, like so:
        Fee, fi, fo, fum, animatus, animatum.
        (The church bell ceases)

PHIPS: I am late to church; I can't comprehend
      Your seventeen.

(ENTER MARY WITH THE GOVERNOR'S BREAKFAST ON A TRAY AND EXITS)

CALEF: You'll not go to church, Phips!
      Death is not set at seventeen, it's no goal,
      No stopping place, no haven. Ambition
      Presides and where sits that sits menace,
      Pride, intimidation and the law in pain.
      Is it no cuff to scruple's better side,
      No slap to reason, no stitch in virtue,
      Yes, or burden to your harvest conscience,
      That law is God and God law? That's slavery!
      I sailed here for freedom! No precept, sir,
      But life! I would believe in Zeus and Rhea,
      Brahma, Krishna and the cow if so free—

PHIPS: *(Eating)* That would get you the brand of heretic
      Quickly, and well earned, I should speculate.

CALEF: If you please, sir, savor the seventeen
      With breakfast, and drink the minister,
      Burroughs, with your coffee.

PHIPS: You've had breakfast?

CALEF: No, Phips, nor do I want any, thank you.

PHIPS: Then, please, do not design against my own,
    But let me finish for church, if you please.
    Reverend John Burroughs! I heard him preach.

CALEF: To be hanged on schedule tonight without help.
    It will make a holiday for Europe's Jews
    When they hear it. The man's wife fled Boston
    Leaving their offspring, Satan's own children,
    To fend as able. It brings calumny,
    Disorder and mistrust. It's inquisition,
    Pure, simple and unadorned. Do end it,
    Sir.

PHIPS: Quite, end it and go to church, should I?
    Say no and yes to my belief in one day,
    One breath? I cannot.

CALEF: You believe in witches?

PHIPS: Do you in evil?

CALEF: Wrong, yes.

PHIPS: Witches do wrong,
    Therefore are possible.

CALEF: Seaman's logic, sir.

PHIPS: Call it what you will; evil lives, Calef.
    (Finished, standing)
    I am off to church now. Do excuse me.

CALEF: I have a long plea; it will not permit
      Of church.

PHIPS: I am late, Calef; long pleas wait.
      (Looks for his Bible)

CALEF: Do not turn your back on mankind to face God,
      I plead. Be civil, civilized and clement,
      Not dogmatic, schedule's sparrow, flighty
      And immune.

PHIPS: I am in flight already;
      I cannot find my Bible. Whose money here?

CALEF: *(Bolts the door, stands not far from it.)*
      Yours.

PHIPS: Mine?

CALEF: Yes, yours.

PHIPS: It is not mine. How did it...?

CALEF: I put it there. It will buy admission
      To the next hangings.

PHIPS: Mary!Mary!

(ENTER MARY)

      Help me to find my Bible; I am late.

MARY: On the table where I put it, sir. Oh! Now there is money.

PHIPS: Mister Calef, I am treated with a grin
　　　　And too much mockery by you of late.
　　　　Explain, sir. Why do you throw the bolt
　　　　On my door, leave money on my table,
　　　　Discourage me from church, risk my anger
　　　　And jeopardize your own true, good, standing
　　　　Here in Boston? Answer me all of that.
　　　　No, I beg you, pass it all by,
　　　　And procure my Bible! I am late to church.

(EXIT MARY)

CALEF: May I go with you?

PHIPS: 　　　　　　　　　　No, you may not.
　　　　You would embarrass God and me, both.
　　　　So, my Bible.

CALEF: 　　　　　Sir, please—

PHIPS: 　　　　　　　　　　　　　My Bible!

CALEF: For Godsake, hear me! I'm no petition
　　　　For a land quarrel, business contract,
　　　　Appointment, favor or like, but human life!
　　　　I plead to live! Flesh! Bone and gristle! Blood!
　　　　Tears and sorrow! Loss and bereavement!
　　　　Act and regret! A damned confusion
　　　　That is mocking us all!

PHIPS: My Bible!

CALEF: Time is life, and life time. Ignore time,
            Crush life! It's most godly and religious
            Of you.

PHIPS: My Bible!

CALEF: I will take my chances.
            It's in the fireplace.

PHIPS: *(Retrieves it, dumb with rage, fear, disbelief)*
                        Well, this is it, alright.
            Why there? Why there, do you say?

CALEF: I dropped it.

PHIPS: So far back, to the chimney wall? The swift
            Was gone from her nest and she is hatching.
            The binding is cracked in two.It was thrown!

CALEF: I had a fit against it.

PHIPS: A fit, you say?
            It was given by the King with his hand
            To me just four years hence, signed by him;
            "To my erstwhile governor, Mister Phips;
            Graciously, King James." It's irreplaceable.

CALEF: My true regrets, sir. In it is something
            Of witchcraft; thou shalt not permit a witch
            To live. It lashes. There is more within

Of witchcraft than in the Hebrew text,
Insertions made to satisfy James' touch
With demonology. This goads me, too.

PHIPS: Why, how do you know this?

CALEF: I know it.

PHIPS: True, how?

CALEF: Through a friend.

PHIPS: A Hebrew wife, is it?

CALEF: Yes.

PHIPS: Why in the fireplace, though? That's deviltry.
        Sure. And bolt my door. Swear in God's name.
        Say you dropped it; confess under pressure.
        Criticize translation. It lashes, you say.
        Bar my way to church, Mister Calef.

(ENTER MARY)

MARY: You are past late, Governor Phips, sir.

PHIPS: I will be absent today. You keep clear
        Of this room, woman, I am not sure who
        This guest is, for certain.

(EXIT MARY)

Indeed, you do
Take chances. Do you know your commandments,
Mister Calef? The Devil will stumble;
Christians name them off.

CALEF: I know them backward, sir.

PHIPS: I will hear them forward.

CALEF: Thou shalt—

PHIPS: True, I know you know them. I am swollen
          Into disbelief, at pettiness outraged,
          Caught up in fashion, quick envisioning.
          Temper sprung of doubt. The disease is on me.
          Is this how it begins?

CALEF: How, root and trunk.

PHIPS: And branches to hanging.

CALEF: From where the leaves fall nightly,
          Mere victims of an ill wind.

PHIPS: Oh, Heaven; why, why, in such a torrent?
          I do not fathom it, no penetration
          Make for reason. I will beg your pardon
          For my presumption and poisoned mind.
          It is all too much. I, myself, submitted
          To it. Shame and discredit to me.
          Hanged if I was ever blacker than now,
          More disfigured than my own sightless eyes,

Seeing, yet not seeing, having vision
Only of light and dark, as does a mole.
Accuse a man of magic, think him rank
And minion of Satan! It is dizzy,
Groundless and derisive riddance taken
Of unstable fear. I know you for a man
And call you evil. What dread is that?

CALEF: Anxiety does convoy dry belief
    Through numerous seas and past many ports,
    Down endless straits, up various rivers,
    Anchors round in bay and estuary, and
    Does protect its produce with devotion,
    Sir. Still, should prow ram hull or broadside
    During some maneuver or at nightwatch,
    Anxiety the rammer or the rammed,
    It's belief will take in water, heed me,
    From the damage.

PHIPS: Well, you ram my faith, Calef,
    Throw away my Bible, impale my attacks
    On thorn like loggerhead shrikes do their prey.
    It's most devilish but not deviltry,
    I must admit.

CALEF: Now, what if there are no witches.

PHIPS: I confess it possible.

CALEF: And no Devil.

PHIPS: Why, then, no God, either. Theology
        Is out the window.

CALEF: And fresh air in, Phips.
        Break off that insulation of the mind
        Which warps and crumples all within its coil.
        Make yourself rid of witches and devils,
        Child-bearing virgins, miracles, marvels,
        Stupefaction of thought. Let the mind breathe!

PHIPS: Hit elsewhere, for on my soul, it is all
        I have.

CALEF: Believe, but envision the world,
        And be drawn out. It needs you.

PHIPS: I beg you,
        Do not use my wisdom on me all at once.
        It is too much for one sitting. Be patient.
        Ease me into it. But not, do not, attack
        My faith; it is set and unbreakable.

CALEF: Good, sir, I will respect your faith as you do
        Mine, a fair exchange.

PHIPS: But you seem to have none.

CALEF: And by mine is your imbued with magic.

PHIPS: Knowing nothing else to say of it, then,
        I will respect your faith, whatever it is.
        Now, what more?

CALEF: The business?

PHIPS: That kept me from church.

CALEF: Sir, I have begun a book on these trials
        Concerned with witchcraft, writing when I can,
        And am not in a court, on horse, at work,
        Or petition raising. I am half way,
        But not yet started. I just recently
        Caught wind of Boston's newest sufferer,
        One Margaret Rule, a girl not eighteen,
        Who demonstrated wildly one Sunday
        In church. Not any church, mind you, but one
        That goes presided over by a sphinx
        To witchcraft, knowing all or near all,
        Writes more on demonology and speaks
        No less than seven languages.

PHIPS: Why, Mather.

CALEF: Right, Cotton Mather whose father, Increase,
        Presidents our Harvard College.
        He accompanied the girl to her house,
        Followed by some coterie of close friends,
        Of which I made myself a dark member.
        There in the front room of the girl's small home
        Some women swore they scented brimstone.
        I smelled nothing, said so meekly but plainly,
        And the noses quick gave away to doubt
        And the mouths to silence. The girl Rule wafted
        Into fits, convulsions, spoke of being damned.
        She was then, to my amazement, undressed

To a trim waist and, before my stunned eye,
Caressed from neck to navel, over breasts,
The nipples played with, and all.

PHIPS: Yes, this is touching to relieve spirits.

CALEF: It relieved frustration, few spirits,
     For the girl was in ecstasy and joy.
     The crowd, some sailors, some coffee house men,
     Had carnival and whore house in a ragout.
     Still more men stroked to relieve her spirits;
     Women could not touch her. She was pat on it.
     When, as luck would have it, my time came,
     She fell limp, relieved, and ready for bed
     With her pick of the strokers, and all left
     But one who got her, I take it, at her
     Maximum temperature.

PHIPS: A moral here not too deeply buried.

CALEF: It's that our prosecutors are all fraud.
     Do they not know that the girls seek love
     And attention, short rations in Boston,
     Andover and Salem, and due their age?
     The Puritan has made firm progress
     In his colony, in church and in heart.
     But latter will not function made too hard.
     So says my book, too.

PHIPS: You will come to grips
     With Mather.

CALEF: True, and will scissor him.
    Release our witches, sir, I beg you.

PHIPS: Release I cannot; that is Stoughton's trust.
    He conducts court here.

CALEF: You are Governor,
    Mister Phips; Stoughton is your deputy.

PHIPS: I cannot embarrass the man to quit.

CALEF: You have questioned witches' reality.

PHIPS: I do that; question does not make fact, though.

CALEF: But you did free John Alden on his name,
    Reputation and good birth.

PHIPS: Come, come, now.
    I knew him to be no witch. My maid, either.

CALEF: Or myself Devil, by the same credentials.

PHIPS: Were you a staunch Devil, Robert Calef,
    Or his diplomat, or witch, or mere elf,
    I would pack me off to England today,
    Due to no good measures available
    Against you here.

CALEF: The rich escape, the poor hang.

PHIPS: I am not accountable for private use
         Of private funds.

CALEF: Oh, yes, if they halt justice.

PHIPS: Man, I had thrown out spectral evidence!

CALEF: Half measures for a full conscience, sir,
         A pacifier, what the Jew calls schnoola.

PHIPS: Look here, Calef, and may my God be judge,
         What I did in Salem by my edict
         Was, in effect, to strip and close the court,
         His court, on my own deputy's head.
         Now, now, you ask me, take off the head.
         Greed is a galleon's hold and dark. Forget,
         Forget, this anger and contempt for law.

CALEF: Finish it or be rightly damned! You scratch
         Like a cricket, conscienceless, hind legged
         And alone. As I have respect remaining,
         Do it! You've deliberated, do it!

PHIPS: I will, and shall try to reassemble,
         In some time, what pieces you have made of me
         In faith and body, soul and poor foresight.
         I will end it, as it must have begun,
         With a word. If you please, Mary!

CALEF: A decision envied even before
         Its execution. My grateful thanks, sir.

(ENTER MARY)

PHIPS: Bring me our pious sheriff out of church.

MARY: Out of church, sir?

PHIPS: Yes, and here.

MARY: Right away, sir.

PHIPS: With or without his bible.

(EXIT MARY)

CALEF: It gives the morning of a bright new day
    New hope, bright promise, green security.
    My repeated gratitude, more thanks yet.
    Ovation fills the heart.

PHIPS: And the bolt is off
    My door; I like that more than I can tell you.

CALEF: Reason will enter on contest's heels;
    What pity it's not built into the toe.

PHIPS: It is not constructed in the toe
    Because it would gain no notice there;
    Our steps into life are more impulsive
    Than reason will allow, thus passion rules
    And thinking counsels. Therefore, our good thoughts,
    Sometimes, no often, late, are found behind
    By some few steps, or, as appears here,

In yet some other's shoes. So energy,
Devotion, blind and passionate, all myself,
Got cornered here behind a locked door.
So they were your toes, sir, your energy
And strength, ruthless persistence, that wore down
My heels to a new awareness, not your thinking
For I did entertain those same thoughts.

CALEF: I must ride promptly on those well heeled thoughts.

PHIPS: Good, Calef. The shoe is comfortable.

CALEF: But out there pinches. Look out your window
At some deputized buffoons making off
With the maid.

PHIPS: Well, let them go.

CALEF: Go, sir?

PHIPS: Never could I stop them; I am worn out.
Indeed, outrun, outreasoned and outplayed.
You go to church for our sheriff.

CALEF: I will.

PHIPS: Interrupt doxology, sermon, psalm,
Whatever, but do bring him out with haste.

CALEF: Then I will go to Salem with the news.

PHIPS: Yes, I would have that. And written out, too.
    (Goes to table to write)

CALEF: All abuse aside, sir, I must favor you
    Among men. Notwithstanding heels and toes,
    What new footwear caused you to shift your thought?

PHIPS: What everyman has if you an penetrate
    To it: Conscience. Will I ever be blessed
    Again, do you think?

CALEF: Yes, if you write fast
    And let me loose. The ropes are up in Salem.

(EXIT CALEF)

(2)

A frog pond. The cart is already unhitched that has chained inside it John Proctor, Burroughs, and Rebecca Nurse, two men and a woman. Stoughton, Parris and the girls are present, Bayles, Hogg and Mobley. The latter sounds the bell intermittently throughout the scene. Frogs are heard from a short distance.

BAYLES: *(Reporting to Stoughton)* The ropes are all up, the people
       waiting, sir. We have kept 'em the other side of the trees like you
       said.

STOUGHTON: Fine, Mister Bayles, you have organized well.
       We have waited long enough for these three.
       Good Reverend Parris, I do lament
       The time it takes legality's procedures
       To take off heads. It has been a dull month
       Of legal claim and worthless counterclaim,
       Investigation and pure molestment,
       From Boston by our truculent Calef.
       But while he now rides a well-lathered horse
       At mane-mangling speed for this holy place,
       He is late, late before arrival even;
       Our early scheduling of the event
       Foxes his timing and gives us Burroughs
       And two more principal witches as well.
       (Goes to inspect, off left)

PROCTOR: *(To Burroughs)* They must be part Roman to watch such
                                    sport.

BURROUGHS: Keep charity, Proctor.

PROCTOR: And lose my head.

BURROUGHS: How fare you, Rebecca?

REBECCA: I can stand to it.

STOUGHTON: *(Returning)* Mister Hogg, to the other bough with
                                                    that rope.

HOGG: *(Goes off to accomplish this)* Right away.

STOUGHTON: Abigail and Ann; do you see clearly?

ALL: Yes, we do. Yes. *(Etc.)*

STOUGHTON: Your wife is found to be in pregnancy,
          John Proctor, and will not follow here
          For some time. Go in peace about her.

PROCTOR: Thank the Lord.
          (To Stoughton) Why, your clothes are all black as ink.
          Not a button is white. Your hat buckle's black,
          And your shirt. Who made you a black shirt?
          And gloves of black kid? Burroughs, see 'em.

STOUGHTON: What should I wear, sir, for solemnity
          But what I have? It is no glad occurrence;
          It is sober, sad, and reverential.
          I dress in the mood.

PROCTOR: Yes, all the way.

STOUGHTON: There is a man in Boston, Proctor,
          Seeking reprieves for all of those condemned—
          Much in contradiction to our court's statutes—
          But should he succeed, he will do it late,
          For the hemp will have had you. Ready now.

BURROUGHS: I do have last words for all of us,
          And would address the people, Stoughton.

STOUGHTON: What, speak for all?

BURROUGHS: I would.

STOUGHTON: Why, Goody Nurse,
          Would you speak for yourself or let your name fall
          From his lips? Do you know the man's crime?

NURSE: I
          Have said all.

STOUGHTON: You, Proctor?

PROCTOR: Oh, yes.

STOUGHTON: Surely?

PROCTOR: Yes, in charity I will keep shut.

STOUGHTON: John Proctor, protect your good name, man.

PROCTOR: What name, sir? When you finished with it,
      I had none worth guarding. He speaks for me.
      Let us hear you, Reverend Burroughs, loudly.

STOUGHTON: Unshackle him, and let us hear his song. *(Bayles*
      unshackles Burroughs, takes him to upstage right where the
      minister faces the Puritan crowd at down stage right. He will exit
      upstage right.)

BURROUGHS: I here submit myself before God,
      My sole judge and witness to my innocence,
      That in Salem we are shamed and broken
      Most disconsolately. Here now come these
      Souls carted to an oaked and crested hill
      By night, in frogging time, for being loosed
      Like insects from their natural domain.
      We are reduced, do you hear, to the fly,
      Ephemeron, and dwell in croaking places.
      If it is but one more step to Hades,
      I should think we are too largely gathered,
      For there is jeopardy in crowds that surge,
      Move their flanks to change their view, regroup
      And gravitate to satisfy all senses.
      So, walk carefully, therefore, according
      To belief. Slip not into the frog pond,
      I urge you. Or, if you are well-reasoned,
      Thinking people who can know the limits
      Of the pond, where it begins and leaves off,
      Is safe and unsafe to step—why, go
      One step further in the mind, then,
      Say to me, Burroughs, do not afright us
      With your flabby images. We know ground

246791114

From water, solid from liquid, and real
From unreal. It's heroic of you, man,
To chortle and gossip on your innocence
Before God, but we have solid proof,
Say it, real and solid proof that you conspired
With the Devil. Then hold it up to this face,
That I may see it; and bring me, please, no shapes.
For we three attest in unit concord
We know no witches or their springing place
Or of their existence, indeed do doubt
Their very plausibility.
Your Dutch philosophers deny them.
They pass them off as figments of the mind;
Yet do they affirm God, yet do they worship
And yet be guided by his same commandments.
Still do they praise the Holy Virgin,
Confirm that Christ did heal in the cities,
Drove avarice and greed from out the temples,
Was crucified and resurrected.
But they do say no to witches!
The common frog has been dissected there
And found unharmed and uncontaminate
By Satan's power. What d'you say of that,
If true? What probity and wisdom, then,
Hold here if frogs are surely not devout
But harmless, too? Neighbors, fellow clergy,
It's Rebecca Nurse, John Proctor, and I
Who, minus superstition, cling on yet!
Empty yourselves of myth and question your faith;
It will have been shaken to the bone!
Yet here are they of witchcraft empty
And of God full, abiding your concepts

Of their guilt or innocence. So are they,
Judged by you, still cherished by their Maker.
It will tear a hole in Heaven the day
They hang, and if this is it, let it, say I,
Be the moment, also. Brutal actions
Plead you sweep, dart, and be done.

(A general sound of censure for the event is heard from the crowd, single displeasures as "I back off it", "No more", "All good people, I have said so", "Free them", "I will listen to a minister to a judge anytime", *but no single voice comes of it, no leadership. Officers look to Stoughton for direction.)*

STOUGHTON: Foolish is it, and most improvident
That at such a time you would seek God's wrath
By putting trust in such a one as he
Who has disgraced the cloak of the clergyman
Everywhere. Deceit and venom cover him;
Vulgarity, contempt, are hid within.
He does burn a mean flame where he takes you.
Disavow him! Your chances take with God!
Boot him out and speak for yourselves
In quiet and respectable tones.
This man's tongue can curve around a tree;
No fly can follow it. What d'you think there?
I have heard him preach in Boston,
Lie in Salem, and now you would entrust him
To dissemble further yet with God!
It is reckless, I beg you consider.
Vindicate yourselves and then disown him!
(To the crowd) They will hang in Hell or here, God choosing
Whether you turn your backs, drop out your eyes,
Give inattention to your commandments,

Fall asleep afoot.Send God to Hell
To hang them up, will you? Neglect your work?
Are we all whoremasters here, giving girls
Their pats and winks, coyly placating them,
While pimps make of crime a public dance?
Damnation and dogs be your company
Hereafter!

BURROUGHS: We are innocent by law!

STOUGHTON: They are innocent as pigs made to pork!

PROCTOR & NURSE: Innocent!

STOUGHTON: Yes, by my God, my Bible is iron!
          I have had enough! It is savaging time!
          Unshackle them!

BURROUGHS: Madman and abject fools!
          (*The two in the cart are released of irons and led off, Burroughs
          with them during Stoughton's speech.*)

STOUGHTON: Devil's underworld has raised itself a notch
          This night! Beware, people. When preachments come
          In too hot, heavy, and unsurpassed guile
          It's best remembered of this eloquence
          That Satan's make-up comes in many hues,
          That he is best in mimicry of God
          And making real things out of seeming!
          Do not discard courage, take a stouter heart,
          For you can hear no minister at all
          In him, but frogs and Dutch philosophers.

It's pure cacophony, the drool and spit
Of necromancy, mouthing, simpering
At Christian justice! Ready; it's best done quick.
Collar each Satanic dog and drop out
The traps! Let them perish! Drop out the traps!

(Stoughton watches, with the children, high into the oaks, with granite sobriety. The curtain slowly falls, or lights slowly dim.)

(3)

Salem prison, Elizabeth Proctor's cell next to Tituba's. Elizabeth holds a small child in her lap.

ELIZABETH: Now another day in Salem prison,
       With most signs pointing to no short limit
       On our time. It is close upon a month,
       Now, one whole month, Tituba, since I have had
       An hour of sun. The child will perish
       Surely. It's damp, musty, and mold on walls
       Is everywhere. A mother yoked to child
       And witchcraft jointly, husbandless and poor,
       Is no rare thing, though, no more bent than others.
       Others as them are hanged and dead, like my John.
       Oh, God, what a man you took and what strength,
       What truth, what poised humility, what pride
       Without conceit, vision without pageant,
       Faith cut loose of doubt, and took it all.
       I remember him. I do covet thoughts,
       The faded ribbon from a prized and empty box.

TITUBA: What name, have you decided, will you give
       To the babe?

ELIZABETH: John Proctor, Tituba,
       As I live by his love.

TITUBA: Then will John Proctor
       Live and flourish as it is God's, and my, wish.

ELIZABETH: Though the original is Heaven sent
        His image lives.

TITUBA: Folks have the bellies full.

ELIZABETH: I hope so. When the judges found it hard
        To hang us fast enough, when some died
        In prison, I heard they let some few escape.
        This may have been noticed by the people.

TITUBA: It was noticed.

ELIZABETH: When they took Sarah Good—

TITUBA: Oh, say nothing. I named her, Sarah Good.
        I named her, and the fear is in me yet
        For it. She, poor one, did damn me proper
        With the stem of her pipe, like so, like so—
        Night following night and day after day.

ELIZABETH: She did pardon you with a grunt, though,
        When she left. Why, they hanged her for contempt,
        Was all.

TITUBA: And went puffing to the gallows,
        Her chin high, but higher yet her nose.
        I hanged her.

ELIZABETH: No more than she hanged me, I think.
        No more than she was guilty for the death
        Of John. What will persecuted ones do,
        Annoy one another, act the predator,
        Accuse when accused? It's natural.

TITUBA: It is sick, it's weak. And I was the full start
       And course of suffering, both map and chart.

ELIZABETH: Console, woman, console; the girls had lured
       Your show to their convenience early.
       You pointed the way; they took the direction.

TITUBA: I never did trust them. The starched hussy
       Abigail, mocked and cut jokes, flaunted
       Cleverness and, to the end, accused me,
       Me, Tituba, to be the Salem witch.
       I foretold the thing, prophesied it;
       Face of God in Salem mud, I said,
       So it came on hard after, and the ruts
       Were deep all year. It was a fool's stunt
       That killed your husband!

ELIZABETH: Those who believed were gulled.

TITUBA: Tituba, the fool.

ELIZABETH: My dear John, husband.

TITUBA: Tituba, the fool.

ELIZABETH: My husband, John.

TITUBA: (Softer) Tituba, the fool.

ELIZABETH: My love, my pride.

TITUBA: (Whispered) Tituba, the fool.

ELIZABETH: Who is gone. *(Both Weep)*

(ENTER HOGG AND CALEF)

HOGG: Here y' are, sir.

CALEF: Do you have the keys?

HOGG: Right here.

CALEF: Well, what is the wait?
          Release them.

HOGG: Now begging your pardon, sir, but there is more—

CALEF: More be damned; you have the order.

HOGG: I do, sir, but in Salem the prisoner must stand the cost of his keep before he is freed, or she, whichever the case. There's no money from the assembly for jail expenses. So the food gets charged, and the men who do the guarding, and the shackles even. It's an expense in time and money to all the good people to keep a jail, and if relatives or friends or somebody don't pay their stay here they must stay on. And rot, for my money. No pay, no freedom, is the law.

CALEF: Here, take this, then.

HOGG: Not sufficient for one of them, sir. They have large accounts.

CALEF: But they are innocent.

HOGG: Don't matter. Those pay as well. If a man takes a room at an inn and sleeps on the floor, not abed, he gets charged the same price, don't he?

CALEF: Compute the sum and bring it to me.

HOGG: Right sir.

(EXIT HOGG)

CALEF: Stoughton's zeal has taken your good husband,
Woman, for which my tears apologize,
But you know this will mean freedom for you.
The Governor has pardoned all. It's over,
Good sense migrates in with an early spring.

ELIZABETH: Who are you, sir?

CALEF: A latecomer, madam,
Whose conscience bleeds, who never suffered
As you have and do; my condolences.

ELIZABETH: Is it well reasoned to think we are free?

CALEF: By pardon legally, but more by fair play
And propriety which, by now, to you
Should sound like foreign phrases, comely talk,
With a part from brow to skull top most suspect.
But it's given by a repentant state,
Call it any such way you might prefer.
The witch hunts are over, all are pardoned.

TITUBA: I know the man and cannot quite place him.
        Ahhh, he healed my face, and sent me a doctor,
        Gave me beer when I was thirsty. On the hunt!
        Your name is Mister Calef! God have mercy;
        Oh, sir, let me serve you. Let Tituba
        Be yours till death! If I'm freed, do let me serve!

CALEF: Elizabeth Proctor, you are called for
        By a cousin in Beverly, poor in means
        Though rich in ways, and who much loves you.

ELIZABETH: Sir, sir, I will repay you. My John,
        Though dead, would have it done. He reviled debt.

CALEF: Now is no time for incurring debts.
        It's for righting wrongful, unfair, records.
        Live, be womanhood, no keeper of books
        And tables, columns and pride Puritan.
        Do live once more; for your good husband live,
        And child. And for self not lastly.
        Come, be loving to nature, kind to man,
        Let the world be redefined in man's wonder
        Of it, letting ignorance take exile,
        For the spectral time of frogs is over.
        Now for our sublime misunderstanding
        Of the frog, he holds it not against us.
        He, as we do, craves his meal and short life
        And harbors, I assure you, no spirits,
        No shapes, no malice and less awareness
        Of ourselves than we do of him. In brief,
        Make of it a world, whatever makes it,
        And be full and done.

(ENTER HOGG)

HOGG: Here, y'are sir. The sum at two shillings, sixpence, weekly. It's a figure of some amount.

CALEF: Will you take a note?

HOGG: Yes, sir.

CALEF: *(While Hogg unlocks)* Mister Hogg, do you have a family?

HOGG: I do, and all saints, too, God bless 'em.

CALEF: I expect good Christians everyone.

HOGG: By the book, sir.

CALEF: Ah, well, I do give them my blessings, too.
There must be reprieve on both sides, don't you think?

HOGG: What, sir?

CALEF: Oh, it all began with a question, too,
For which there seems no positive adieu.
But I will hope till I am out of hope.

THE END

Sautee and Nacoochee

A Georgia Tragedy

Robert Manns

The story of Sautee and Nacoochee springs from the north Georgia mountains and, by whatever means, from the prior inhabitants of, or visitors, to the area. While simulated parchment documents are offered of the lovers' lives and as a genuine burial mound is described as the final resting place, I have also heard that a visiting University of Georgia professor with a sense of puckish humor contrived the fable while dwelling on the town names, Sautee and Nacoochee. That information I gathered from a museum guard in Helen who was present on the professor's field trip.

Never mind. The story, true or figured, approximate or totally contrived, is so simple and direct that streets in Atlanta are named for the pair and, probably in more places than one, similar honors are paid.

The story goes, as close as I can figure it, that Sautee, a Chickasaw, was journeying through Cherokee land. He stopped at a large oak, caught the attention of lovely Nacoochee, and the two fell bow over arrow in love. But when Chief Wahoo of the Cherokees found his daughter entrapped by a Chickasaw, he had Sautee thrown to his death from Mount Yonah. Nacoochee, freeing herself from her father's grasp, jumped after him. The chief, overcome with remorse, then buried the two lovers together in a burial mound.

Postulating the legend to be true, it has the force of a moral tale. If not true, it still has the force of a moral tale. So its verity is hardly the most important thing about it, to my mind., because if false, it still makes its way out of someone's need to tell it.

Obviously, then, I also have the need to tell it. Funny how from generation to generation our basic requirements of life remain so close together.

The Author

Cast of Characters

SAUTEE, TOM

An Indian Chickasaw full blood at about, say thirty—less or more—strong bodied, handsome, articulate. He is an amateur astronomer and telescope sales person working for his father's company. He carries the environmental awareness of an Indian, love of the land and celestial bodies.

NACOOCHEE, ROSEMARY

A striking woman of a few years less than Sautee, descended from a full blood Cherokee line, articulate and strong willed.

PETER

An elderly full blood Indian, philosophical, grandfather to Sautee.

HORACE

Father to Sautee. Owner of Lightfoot Industries, an optical company for sky scopes, spotting scopes, binoculars, etc., an erudite businessman.

MELINDA

A still lovely mother of Sautee, kind and proud of her environment.

MAUDE	Mother of Nacoochee, a bit worrisome but interested, too interested, in the fate of Nacoochee.
FATHER COUGHLIN	A cleric.
MEREDITH	An Indian worker for Lightfoot Industries.
PAUL	The same, younger perhaps.
ESTELLE	A prostitute.
TIKI	
	Summer camp solicitors.
JOE	

SCENE ONE

The Lightfoot homefront is largely stone with a generous front door and walk leading to it between two floral areas. Between the flowers and house is a small recreational patio occupied by Meredith and Paul.

Late afternoon of a sunny day in a mountain township in north Georgia, in an outskirt of the town where there are monastic homes on large estates. Two men of Indian heritage, plainly dressed, sit drinking beer.

MEREDITH: That's good mead, Paul.

PAUL: Mead got honey; that's beer.

MEREDITH: You're right, I forgot. You're absolutely right. Little old brewer downtown knows his stuff, don't he? You ever drank better?

PAUL: No, Meredith, I guess I never.

MEREDITH: Then—(*Raises his glass in toast*)

PAUL: (*Meeting his glass*) (*Toast*).

MEREDITH: (*Stunned*) Hell, you cracked my glass.

PAUL: (*Complacent*) I did?

MEREDITH: I believe you did.

PAUL: Sorry.

MEREDITH: *(Examining the glass further)* There's the crack.

PAUL: Sure, enough.

MEREDITH: Not really much of a crack, though.

PAUL: Meredith?

MEREDITH: Yeah?

PAUL: The beer is beginning to make my head dizzy.

MEREDITH: You like it?

PAUL: I sure do.

MEREDITH: Have some more. *(Pouring)* It's fine ale. When Tom Lightfoot buys booze for his friends, he makes sure it's the best. That's because he has the best friends.

PAUL: Who?

MEREDITH: Us, you fool.

PAUL: Look, here comes Mr. Lightfoot home from work. I saw him drive in a minute ago. He's the kind of daddy Tom deserves, all right. Look, the stride on that man.

MEREDITH: Proud walk of a proud man. Hello, Mr. Lightfoot!

ENTER MR. LIGHTFOOT FROM RIGHT

LIGHTFOOT: Meredith, Paul, I see you're into your afternoon libations as usual. I wish I could join you. Is Tom in?

PAUL: Yessir, he's in the back looking at one of the new telescopes you had sent to the house.

LIGHTFOOT: Good. I'll want to look at that myself. Enjoy yourselves, but do use the paths between the flower beds.

PAUL: Yessir, yessir. *(Raising his glass in a toast)*Health to you, sir.

EXIT MR. LIGHTFOOT INTO THE FRONT DOOR

MEREDITH: Careful you don't crack him wide open with that toast. Have you been walking on the flowers?

PAUL: Not me, no, not me. You?

MEREDITH: I don't tread on flowers, Paul, I do the ridges. Always walk high.

PAUL: Well, I'm high right where I am, sitting down. The better the beer, the higher I go, too.

MEREDITH: *(Looking off)* Whoa, who's this coming from the street? Oh, what a lovely by this eye, and this eye is all I need. I may need some restraints.

PAUL: Oh, smokes, what a beauty, all right. Should we button our sleeves? My hair okay?

MEREDITH: Just look your usual rabbity self. She's not for you, not for me.

PAUL: Nature commits more crimes than it'll admit, I say.

ENTER ROSEMARY ABBOT, a very lovely young woman.

ROSEMARY: Good afternoon. Is the owner of the home in?

MEREDITH: Well, mam, if I told you I was the owner, would that help?

ROSEMARY: Why, yes, it would.

MEREDITH: Well, I'm not, so I guess I can't help you. Not that way, anyway.

ROSEMARY: Would you be so kind? I would like to speak to the owner.

MEREDITH: *(Playfully, teasingly)* Gee, let me see.

ROSEMARY: Extend yourself, sir.

MEREDITH: *(Liking the play)* Oh, you hear, Paul, the lady wants extension? *(He slouches in his chair, extending his upper body and legs)* Now I got extension.

ROSEMARY: Oh, my mother warned me that gentlemen could be otherwise, but never to cast blame until proof was evident.

MEREDITH: Why, is it proof when just evident? Hey, Paul, where's the nearest law school? We got a thing going here. *(Standing, Paul behind him)* We're just hired hands here, Mam, and Mr. Lightfoot just went into the rear of the house where his son is looking at a new 'scope. *(Joking)* By now he's probably taken it away from him. I'll call his son for you. *(Calling)* Hey, Tom. Tommy!

ROSEMARY: Thank you, sir.

MEREDITH: Please don't call me sir, mam; I'll be asking for a raise, if you do.

ROSEMARY: Any preferences?

MEREDITH: Oh god, Paul, she's too fast for me. Let's sit down. *(They do. Meredith calls again)* Tom! *(To Rosemary)* You like a beer?

ROSEMARY: No, thank you.

ENTER FROM THE FRONT DOOR, TOM LIGHTFOOT

TOM: Heard you the first time, Meredith. *(Looks at Rosemary, who looks at him, with mutual approval. No one speaks, moves. Finally—)* How do you do?

ROSEMARY: How do you do?

MEREDITH: Well, that's how they both do, so far. *(Pours both glasses full, they silently toast, clinking glasses)*

TOM: I'm Tom Lightfoot

ROSEMARY: I'm Rosemary Abbott.

PAUL: That's more than Meredith learned, Tom.

ROEMARY: I—My family just moved into the house across from you and would like to invite you and your family to an open house this weekend or next to get acquainted. I hope you can come.

TOM: I believe that's a reversal of form. We just heard—

ROSEMARY: We like to reverse time-honored etiquette.

TOM: Yes, well—

MEREDITH: She's got his tongue. Go, girl.

ROSEMARY: Your home is imposing: have you lived here long?

TOM: Yes, for centuries. The house is built on the site of another that burned some time ago. That was built on the site of a cabin belonging to my forebearers. And that, in turn, was built on the ground of a Chickasaw lodge occupied by my great-great-great grandparents. So, you see, for centuries.

ROSEMARY: And you look so young!

TOM: You're very gracious. A people must follow its livelihood, I suppose. We escaped our tribes removal westward. We moved east, to here, our family's original country. We had the protection of white friends, or so I'm told. Now, due I think to an enterprising father, we're Lightfoot Opticals downtown. We sell optics for up there and down here.

ROSEMARY: Down here?

TOM: Yes. A hawk has eight times our vision. That gives him an advantage of eight magnifications over a man. To get even, to study nature, one has a binocular and to study it over long distances, a spotting scope—so, the earth. We have much to learn about our own planet, also.

ROSEMARY: Oh, I would look forward to learning more, and I hope I will.

TOM: There is so much. Just imagine, if you can, the many years and hard study a student puts into any given field just to find that he's so proficient there that he has become ignorant in many others. He can't raise a responsible child, can't build a house, doesn't drive a car too well, uses his table napkin as a handkerchief and has never even tried to read *Moby Dick*. Well, there you are, the price of concentration, the intensification of one field causing the total loss of others. How do you win, you see? You don't. It's not even a matter of winning. But there is no pleasure in not playing, either. I would like to come to your open house.

ROSEMARY: I hope you will come and bring family.

TOM: Well, I have no family, but I'll ask those I'm family of to come. Will that do?

ROSEMARY: Quite. Oh, yes, quite.

MEREDITH: Now he's got hers.

ROSEMARY: I did the opposite of concentrating because I thought that nearly everyone was doing it and there should be some places in life for the generalist. I went to William and Mary and came out a liberal arts major with a minor in history, American history. Now, can you sell that? No, of course not. But it seemed to put me in position to speak English without too many blemishes, to understand ethics and the wealth of our culture and some good number of doors opened. So, there you are. Or there I am, so to speak. And I like it. I have the freedom and some of the abilities, I believe, to investigate some other things. Do you teach? I don't mean to be forward, but I'm a good student. I take notes.

TOM: Rosemary Abbott, you say.

ROSEMARY: Yes. And—and Tom Lightfoot?

TOM: Yes. I'll be there, happily.

ROSEMARY: We will be more than happy to have you. I'll be—

MEREDITH: Ohmygod, the two way happiness.

TOM: It's my pleasure to meet you, Rosemary.

ROSEMARY: My pleasure—no, my pleasure. *(Tom watches her leave)*

EXIT ROSEMARY LEFT

PAUL: *(As Tom fixes on Rosemary's departure)* You hear that, Meredith?

MEREDITH: Hear it? I wrote it down. *(Inspecting the palm of his hand)* Now, let's see. "I hope you'll come. I'll try, ohmygod, I'll try. You married, boy? No more than you are, I hope, mam. Your name Rosemary, you say? And yours is Tommy Littlefoot? Oh, how cute. Pleasure to meet you. Oh, no, pleasure's all mine. Please, no, mine. No, no, mine, mine." That's what it says here, Paul, 'd I leave anything out?

TOM: You clowns. You buffalo stalkers. You haven't any right to squaws. You opened your little lenses and gaped a bit, no? Well, you should have. By the sun that attends this earth, you should have. You would have seen a galaxy of beauty.

MEREDITH: Oh, spare me the amateur astronomer!

TOM: In her you have the formation of a new star, molecular hydrogen and dust condensing into lumps that contract and unite under their own gravity to become her, a star.

MEREDITH: New stars give off gas, you told me once.

TOM: Forget what I told you once. Remember what I'm telling you now. Before you drive another Lightfoot Industries truck remember that I, Tom Lightfoot, was struck dumb by a visiting angel—

MEREDITH: Star.

TOM: Angelic star, who tore out my heart and impaled it shrike-like on my father's barbed fence.

PAUL: Good grief!

MEREDITH: We only have one truck, Tom, and you said I could take it into Atlanta this weekend.

TOM: Fair, agile, tall, warm. She moves like a mountain lion after game.

PAUL: *(Clucking like a hen in distress)*

TOM: I'll do it, I'll go; it will be a visit to a museum. She's a vision. And what does one do with a vision? Dream it? Forget it, only to remember it again and again? Follow. Find out where it goes.

PAUL: Meredith, he's gone.

MEREDITH: Far. Get some more beer: I think we're in for one.

EXIT PAUL INTO THE PATIO DOOR WHILE TOM, STILL WATCHING THE PATH OF ROSEMARY'S EXIT, SLUMPS WEAKLY INTO A GARDEN CHAIR.

SCENE TWO

An evening the following weekend, the night of the invitation. The scene is the same, but lighted dimly.

TOM: *(Is sitting low in one chair with his feet propped up on another. He is dressed in a suit but casually and has the air of one deep into confusion. He turns slowly, holds his head after slumping forward, returns to a slouch with feet up. He sighs, shakes his head. He is amazed at his distress. Enter Rosemary from right. She is unseen at first and pauses as though waiting for recognition. He turns and squirms to his feet.)* I beg your pardon.

ROSEMARY: I hoped you would come. I suppose I went out on a limb and told several people in the neighborhood Tom Lightfoot would be there. It seems you have quite a reputation for honesty.

TOM: I hope so.

ROSEMARY: And fair play. No enemies but one, and he lives on the other side of town.

TOM: A customer I removed from the store.

ROSEMARY: He was drunk.

TOM: You are informed.

ROSEMARY: I have to be. In the absence of first hand information, one seeks second hand. It was awful that I found myself gathering hand-me-down news. Why didn't you come?

TOM: I was there. You put on a marvelous throw, I'll tell you. The attendance was fantastic. Men were at their handsomest, women coming out of their dresses. Full drinks in every glass and no one staggering. Charity everywhere. It was an opulence that wouldn't let me get comfortable. Then you, my god, then you. That dress, that grace, that—.

ROSEMARY: That what?

TOM: Yes, that what.

ROSEMARY: Are you frightened, Mr. Lightfoot?

TOM: Terrified, Ms. Abbott. Worse, really, more like annihilated, I think. I study the stars, you know, constellations, nebulae and the neatly crafted instruments that reveal them to us and these eyes—these instruments—saw such bright light in a dim room that I was struck dumb. It was a spear when a stone would have done it. So I came back here to twiddle my thumbs and study my fear.

ROSEMARY: To withdraw, they say.

TOM: Same horse, different saddle. It's the force of the blow that stuns, no real pain, mind you. You stagger and lurch and hear the coliseum Romans scream for more.

ROSEMARY: Are you saying—? Is all this in reference to me?

TOM: Oh, no, ma'am. To Orion and his dog after the mutt stole a chunk of his master's other end for foot dragging. Slow to cross the night sky, you see.

ROSEMARY: Orion?!

TOM: You've heard of him?

ROSEMARY: You were not at the party; will you give me a civil answer why?

TOM: Civil, lady, is a matter of private rights; I take the fifth.

ROSEMARY: But why?

TOM: Never hear of him?

ROSEMARY: Who?

TOM: *(Pointing)* Him, up about there. Him, Orion, with one cheek torn and his mind in utter confusion over why the thing of his life should cause him such delicious pain.

ROSEMARY: Well, now, I'm much more confused than he is and without anyone having been around, you know—out of sight.

TOM: Not bitten?

ROSEMARY: I didn't say that!

TOM: I was, honestly, at the party—all of a few minutes, as I said. I was aware of a lot of planetary folks and one celestial being who blinded me.

ROSEMARY: My mother?

TOM: Isn't it a lovely moon drenched night? Imagine how all this soft light, from here to there and so many places we can't even see, comes from that single bulb up there. Lumens inconceivable. Would you like to sit down?

ROSEMARY: I will wrinkle my dress if I do.

TOM: Wrinkle it.

ROSEMARY: *(Sitting)* So you came to the party, after all, and found yourself spooked by its size, I suppose. I was very eager to introduce you to people, but I couldn't find you in any of the closets.

TOM: I was in all of them. I was probably being somewhat unmannerly about leaving, for which I apologize. I haven't any idea of how to behave, really. After all, you're new to me.

ROSEMARY: I think I understand.

TOM: Spare me understanding. I want to be as mysterious to you as the human race is to itself. Don't offer me comprehension, leave me my clothes.

ROSEMARY: Well, as for that—

TOM: I take it back.

ROSEMARY: Am I hearing you say you're so overturned by me that you can't attend a welcoming party, have to withdraw home and consult with the moon on how to keep your mystery and, yet, find yourself willing to shed your suit?

TOM: Yes, yes, or yours.

ROSEMARY: *(Standing)* God help me, I have found an honest man!

TOM: *(The same)* Then you were looking!

ROSEMARY: Hard!

TOM: No wonder I was confused; you bated all your hooks at once. You went silently into the night to arrive early, first light, at the fishpond.

ROSEMARY: Oh, please, Thomas, I hardly think—

TOM: Oh, I know whereof I speak. I know, because I was there waiting for you.

ROSEMARY: Oh, it's not a real world, after all.

TOM: Not if we transcend it, I guess.

ROSEMARY: Are you sure you don't just want to bed with me?

TOM: Just try taking the worms out of the earth and see what you've got left, Rosemary. Bedding the one who makes your head spin isn't the least of human efforts. It takes hope, plan and tactic, the conquest of fear, an explosion of feeling and a night watch of the other's fear and feeling. It takes a fair maneuver, in other words.

ROSEMARY: Oh, why did you have to add the other words.

TOM: Rosemary, I would never take advantage.

ROSEMARY: But are you an astronomer?

TOM: Only enough astronomer to claim to be an optics consultant and vice versa, but reasonably able to name some songbirds, anyway, of our country. Maybe the hawks, too.

ROSEMARY: The country, the land, is important to you, isn't it?

TOM: Those to whom it's unimportant should pack. Our people didn't die trying to protect an empty realm and the white man took it by natural accretion. We understand that now. It could never have been unimportant. Somehow, both sides knew its value. Oh, yes, it's important to me. And now you've made it even more important.

ROSEMARY: Well, I don't think I have ever improved real estate values before, but if that's what I've done here and no one has lost a nearby farm, I'm proud of my work. My father taught me a little about our nefarious tax base. And you say you know your songbirds. That's certainly more than quaint. Maybe you can tell me what that little brown-backed bird is that skulks around bushes and points his tail up as though he was always pointing to something skyward behind him, pointing backwards, kind of.

TOM: Call the Audubon people.

ROSEMARY: Oh, you don't know?

TOM: I do, but won't tell.

ROSEMARY: A pedant is one who preaches more than he practices. If you have no experience with birds, what do you do with them? Dress yourself in their colors, learn the acrobatics of flight from them, sing their songs back at them? Very curious.

TOM: I steal their eggs. Free breakfast.

ROSEMARY: That's illegal.

TOM: I do little illegal things. When I was a boy, I caught beetles in a jar and kept them for study at least a half-hour, then let them go. I knew that little things had to eat as often as possible. How did I know that? I projected, I suppose.

ROSEMARY: Brilliant. And I'm to suppose you learned more about beetles than you did birds.

TOM: Oh, no.

ROSEMARY: Then don't tell me to call Audubon, name my bird.

TOM: I will not. It's clear you only want to know because a convenient situation has presented itself in which you can achieve a small piece of knowledge you otherwise and otherwhere wouldn't give a damn about.

ROSEMARY: Oh, you're profane.

TOM: Never. That was a measurement of your true concern: Less than negligible.

ROSEMARY: And insulting!

TOM: I am always telling people off, especially those who practice casual learning.

ROSEMARY: And egotistical!

TOM: Yes, if I am going to be profane and insulting, I don't want any conscience about it, so I invoke my ego. That's natural and good, because it allows me a still good opinion of myself.

ROSEMARY: Totally imperious!

TOM: Hey, all these names!

ROSEMARY: I want my bird!

TOM: No!

ROSEMARY: Yes!

TOM: Skulks, you say?

ROSEMARY: You heard me.

TOM: *(A beat)* Carolina wren. Just a small member of the natural world that raises its head to you.

ROSEMARY: And tail.

TOM: I forgot the tail.

ROSEMARY: Do you know what you're doing?

TOM: Do you?

ROSEMARY:How certain electricity is when it crackles. I think I liked
you the moment I saw you.

TOM: The same here, but, of course, the faster you ride a horse, the
more care you'd better have, too. But let's not slow down yet.
Good grief, we just got into the saddles.

ROSEMARY: It's so unreal.

TOM: Is the crater of a volcano real to those below? Only when it
erupts. Till then, a wonderfully quiet and benevolent fellow.
We are at the cusp, Rosemary.

ROSEMARY: Aren't there more agreeable cusps in astrology?

TOM: You ask an astronomer that?

ROSEMARY: It seems I've heard—

TOM: There are, it's true. Choose one, if you prefer fables.

ROSEMARY: I prefer you, Tom.

TOM: And I you, Rosemary.

ROSEMARY: It used to snow here, but the climate has changed. And I enjoyed the snow, I don't know why. It was white, very white. It was so, so—composing. Whenever the first flakes fell, people's attentions were arrested, I think. Then, as the flakes grew heavier, they were dazed. And when it continued beyond amazement and the ground took on that lifting and transmuting cover the color of bone, I for one, just became fixed. The dream was on me. If I were indoors, the warmth was suffusing. No other warmth was that comforting. Except this one.

TOM: And not so many lives ago my ancestors blanketed themselves under deerskin or, with luck, buffalo robe. Much less than amazed, they became withdrawn into the need for warmth. This caused, I'm told, withdrawal of all the senses, like a hibernation of the mind till the first melt. They were never as warm as I am now.

ROSEMARY: Time changes us, doesn't it?

TOM: I should say. If we were unchangeable, we might have gotten stuck back on all fours.

ROSEMARY: Then our needs change, I suppose.

TOM: Yes, or should. Think of a world without forgiveness.

ROSEMARY: War.

TOM: But we're somewhere else in time, we two. (They kiss)

ROSEMARY: I find that stirring. I'd like to do it again. (They do)

TOM: It's an awakening.

ROSEMARY: I would hope so.

TOM: Rosemary, there are some Caucasian people who think we Indians all drink whiskey for breakfast and can't drive cars.

ROSEMARY: Well, can you?

TOM: What?

ROSEMARY: Drive.

TOM: Yes, but can't stomach whiskey any time.

ROSEMARY: I think you'll do.

TOM: But it will be your people I'm concerned with. I don't know them. They don't know me. I'm a little frightened of that.

ROSEMARY: First you are frightened of me and now you are frightened of my parents. I have two uncles. Would they scare you? I have two aunts, one rather mousy, the other a war party. You'd be frozen. The war party has a dog, big ol' Boxer, tear your liver out if he didn't melt you first with huge brown eyes. The mousy one has a Poodle.

TOM: I'm concerned, let's say. Many think we were all at Little Big Horn, Custer is their martyr.

ROSEMARY: Oh, dear, the suffering you must have stowed in your quiver. Most Americans confront the Amerindian with a sense of guilt, I think. Sports teams are named for them, cars, foods and weapons are named for them, streets and whole cities. The Indian is in the American culture root and trunk to stay, Tom. What, so I'm a gypsy, you wouldn't love me?

TOM: I would.

ROSEMARY: Chinese?

TOM: Yes.

ROSEMARY: You pass all the tests, but there's no reason for fear at all: I have Cherokee blood from my father, the grandson of a full blood. My name at birth was Nacoochee. We were in Tennessee and Georgia.

TOM: I'm all disbelief. Mine was Sautee. I was supposed to have been born strong and tall as a beech tree, and so it's that tree that I honor.

ROSEMARY: I will be your live oak, content with less height but strong against the wind, Sautee.

TOM: A Cherokee and a Chickasaw. Here's to growing together, Nacoochee.

SCENE THREE

Late night, a street corner in Atlanta. Meredith and a hooker, Estelle. Meredith, drunk, reels.

MEREDITH: How much, my little Atlanta siren?

ESTELLE: I don't do nothing for less than fifty, baby, that's my special for country boys.

MEREDITH: Not bad, fifty cents.

ESTELLE: You're one very funny Indian. What you got?

MEREDITH: Funny hooker, too, wants to know how much in the bank before she robs it. I got what it takes. *(Searching)* Somewhere.

ESTELLE: You're drunk.

MEREDITH: You call three little boilermakers drunk?!

ESTELLE: No, I didn't call three little boilermakers drunk, I called you drunk. You couldn't handle anything like me, honey, look what I got. And you, your pants are coming down over your hips.

MEREDITH: Easier to get to things that way.

ESTELLE: What you got to get to? Let's stop playing games.

MEREDITH: You wanna see?

ESTELLE: Money!! I'm talkin' money, Geronimo!

MEREDITH: *(Searching again for money)* I got a boss and he got a girl and his head's where my money's got to—lost. No, wait, I feel something. You should look like her; you'd be queen of the streetlights. Ah! Shit, bottlecaps.

ESTELLE: Well, I may not look like her but I don't walk the streets with a pocket full of bottlecaps!

MEREDITH: I save them, pitch to the wall, with Paul.

ESTELLE: So the man with the looker pitches bottlecaps with you? Tell him to bring some bread down here, and we'll do a double header.

MEREDITH: No, you turkey, Paul's got less bread than an empty oven, and my boss—you'd have to pay him. *(Still searching)* Now, somewhere—Ah! Ah! Got something.

ESTELLE: A piece of meat, maybe.

MEREDITH: Yea, yea, got that, too. *(Producing)* Look! Twenty!! What's your name?

ESTELLE: Estelle. Dig some more.

Robert Manns

MEREDITH: Bottomed out!

ESTELLE: Come on, then, twenty skins worth.

EXIT BOTH

_____

Robert Manns

MEREDITH: Bottomed out!

ESTELLE: Come on, then, twenty skins worth.

EXIT BOTH

_____

Robert Manns

MEREDITH: Bottomed out!

ESTELLE: Come on, then, twenty skins worth.

EXIT BOTH

_____

SCENE FOUR

The interior of the Lightfoot home, the living room. A simple stone fireplace at left center with a picture of a middle aged Indian woman over it, some filled book shelving at right rear, a sofa, chairs and area rugs. It is evening of a few days later. Present are Horace Lightfoot, Tom's father, his mother, Melinda and Tom's grandfather, Peter.

HORACE: In summary then, Lightfoot Opticals is still competitive with its main northern competitors and still pursues an old American custom of complete service to its customers. We not only serve the nation, thereby, we dignify it in fact, by allowing a customer all the knowledge of a product he can stand. If only our citizenry took the country as seriously as we do our optics, it would be the happiest of nations. And why shouldn't we be? We have it all, I think: Mountains, Great Plains, barrier islands, rivers, floodplain, deserts and more mountains. These States are generously endowed, I tell you, and deserve no less than a respectful people. Since a respectful people are a peaceful people and a peaceful people are a unified one—we have just described the Lightfoot family, mercifully unified. And so I conclude with a philosophical aspect of our business, having covered the mathematics.

MELINDA: I'm comfortable with that. You, father?

PETER: If Horace says so, I guess. My son is a good business head.

HORACE: Oh, hear, hear.

MELINDA: Why, you know it, of course, Horace. People tell you often enough, I see you swell like a peacock.

PETER: Prairie chicken, Melinda.

MELINDA: Sorry, Father.

PETER: I know, because I was one once. The prairie chicken on his lek, you know, booming and puffed up, his sacs in high color. That was me. Then my woman, Horace's mother, got sick and the days and nights got longer. On the last day when I stood by her bed—I've never told you this—I thought I would get into the bed with her and hold her in my arms. But when I looked down, she was gone. I looked over her bed at the wall at the long end of the room. There was no window, nothing on it. I thought this must be how it will be the rest of the way.

MELINDA: When the storm passed, the sky was blue again and there was your son, his son and his mother.

PETER: All made possible from the belly of my Marie. It's true, there is occasional light. But I had seen death before; I will again.

HORACE: There was the light you passed on to a small boy when you gave him a toy telescope and told him to look at the night sky, remember. Another when you taught him mathematics and his attentions were made even more precise my numerology. The two gifts gave us Lightfoot Opticals.

PETER: Oh, yes. *(Bored)*

HORACE: Then, my dear Peter, from your seed and Marie's flower came, after my and Melinda's little germination, our brilliant son, Tom—a gift of no little time. It was, I have to say, a realization made over many moons.

PETER: *(Still bored)* Um-hm.

HORACE: And the short of it is, you made me handsome enough to take our Melinda to wife. All light; stand in it, Peter.

PETER: Tally it all to my Marie.

HORACE: And mine?

PETER: Yes, and yours.

MELINDA: Father—

HORACE: Peter, may we all make an observance together of Marie later this evening?

PETER: A remembrance out of place, you say. Certainly, later, in its place. Though ten months gone is a time hard to order. Very hard.

MELINDA: Father, you're in agreement with Horace's financial report?

PETER: Oh, yes, and glad it's finished, of course.

HORACE: Well, then, another annual pow-wow on the company is concluded and we have gotten to rum time. Isn't it curious how time alone alters complex custom? Time was when the most barbaric tribes of some of us southward practiced cannibalism and thought nothing of it. Now the voice of the squaw is heard in corporate meetings and we're happy to have them. Time makes liars of us all, Father. *(After mention of rum time, Melinda turns right toward the kitchen.)*

EXIT MELINDA

PETER: Not me, son. I hope I can say that I represent and embody the eternal in our lives. What hope is there for an ever-changing world? We long ago discovered the meanings of things and found them valuable. We endorsed them and lived by them. The gods of our fathers became our gods, our women became our sons' mothers, the well made arrow found its mark. Time did not lie to us; it verified us.

HORACE: You think so?

PETER: Well, you credit me, your father, with fortitude and strength, an eye to the thing in front of me with knowledge of who's behind me. You say I gave you those qualities. You say I gave you patience and wisdom. Where do you think those came from, the air? They came from your grandfather, my father, who inherited them from his father. They were a series of absolutes that resisted change through years. You don't get men of rock until generations first observe and understand, then become, the hardened and composed earth themselves. We are from the earth we walk on, due to return to it. you know.

HORACE: I would argue that with Plato, not you.

PETER: Yes, you would—pick on poor Plato.

HORACE: You'd say we, you and I, had not changed?

PETER: Trivial things, nothing substantial. I could return to the humble lodge of our fathers, you couldn't.

HORACE: True, of course.

PETER: Of course.

ENTER MELINDA, *with glasses of rum*

Ah, the unchanged truth in another ancient form. *(Taking his)*

HORACE: Somewhat more refined in the distilling, I might add. *(Taking his)*

PETER: Trivial matter.

MELINDA: I see father and son are at it, again.

HORACE: I suppose till Venus embraces the Pleiades and puts the heavens at peace. *(There is a loud knock at a door beyond the kitchen.)*

MELINDA: I'll get it.

EXIT MELINDA, *we hear her open a door to the outside, Paul's and her voice:*

MELINDA: Come in, Paul.

PAUL: Pardon, ma'm, I just wanted to know where to leave the truck, if Mr. Lightfoot has a preference.

MELINDA: Come in and ask him, Paul.

PAUL: Thank you, ma'm.

ENTER PAUL FOLLOWED BY MELINDA

HORACE: The truck can stay wherever you left it, Paul. And, while you're here, have a little rum, won't you?

PAUL: Yessir, you know I will. I don't mind drinking beer with Meredith but rum's really my drink. One swallow and I can sing, you know. Two, and I can bring the song sparrow off her nest.

HORACE: Yes, I'm sure. Well, where are Meredith and Tom, off hootching it up together?

PAUL: Oh, nossir, more likely off lovin' it up together, I'd think. But not together, nossir, separately I mean, of course. Each with his choice, you know. Meredith's had his head torn off by some woman in town I've never seen and Tom's drunk without a drop over the new neighbor across the way. I think you know who I mean, do you?

HORACE: Well, that accounts for his absence of late and, if he's taken, that's not unhealthy, either. But while you're here would you favor us with a song? Nothing to bring the sparrow indoors, though.

PAUL: Oh, nossir. I mean yessir to the song, no to the bird. I have to keep my priorities straight, don't I? What would you like, Mr. Lightfoot?

HORACE: Do you call it the Six Nations Dance?

PAUL: Yessir, they say the Six Nations Dance. The way I understand it there was six different tribes got together. I didn't know you knew I knew this one. Anyway, maybe the tribes had been fighting over hunting grounds. Maybe they had made a peace. No one knows. When they got together, well, they celebrated and made this dance the Six Nations Dance. It's a "mixed dance," they call it. My brother used to call it a mixed dance.

HORACE: Will you sing it for us?

PAUL: Glad to, but I gotta tell you a bit more here. A six Nations Dance is something like a social dance. That's the one we done all night long with different leaders, I'm told. Story has it that Hayes Lossiah was a good leader. It says Will Pheasant, John Driver was pretty good, John W. Driver and Going Bird, Killing Wolf, too.

HORACE: But you know the words, do you?

PAUL: Oh, yes, know them backward, sir. Just a bit more here: Will Driver used to lead some in my time, Running Wolf Sequoyah, Lloyd Sequoyah. And us younger folks we used to lead a little bit.

HORACE: Do lead, please.

PAUL: Coming to it, sir.

MELINDA: You call it a dance and it's a song?

PAUL: Yes ma'm.

MELINDA: But which is it?

PAUL: Why, it's both, ma'm.

HORACE: They sing and dance at the same time, Melinda, nothing new there. Most of the white entertainers do that today. One or the other's still not enough alone because of the lack of quality alone, I suppose.

PAUL: That's it, Mr. Lightfoot, both together.

HORACE: Well, will you surprise us and sing?

PAUL: Yessir. This is the way the Six Nations Dance goes. *(a pause)* some calls it "Mixed Dance." Call it by either name, I guess.

HORACE: Please sing before it grows another.

PAUL: *(Sings the Six Nations Dance in an abbreviated form.)*
    Yo Ho
    O He Ye o he ye O He Ye o he ye
    we he ye we he we he
    Oh He Ye o he ye O He Ye o he ye
    WOOO
    A no he ya he He ya a (Repeat five times)
    Eg wa ga to si He ya hay
    El la wa E lo she He yah He yah hay
    Gal sta hv tv ni He yah hay
    We Ga ga lo shi He yah hay
    Tsal ga li e He yah hay
    Hah na hvi He yah hay
    Gv na li i hey shi He yah hay
    e no he ye He yah hay
    He no he yv he He yah hay
    A no he yah he He yah hay
    WOOO

PAUL: *(Concluding)* That's it; that's the six Nations Dance. There's more but it would take the rest of the day to sing it.

HORACE: No, no, that's enough, and thank you, Paul.

PAUL: Was it good enough for another nip, sir?

HORACE: Help yourself for the sparrow's sake, then, but don't go near the truck.

PAUL: Yessir and nossir. *(Drinks, licks his lips)* Thank you, Mr. Lightfoot.

EXIT PAUL

MELINDA: So, my child has met with an interest.

HORACE: Your child has met with many interests, Melinda. D'you remember the lady at the lake last summer? The archaeologist who was always digging into his past? The young lady before that who thought Tom's preoccupation with environmental matters was tedious? Women have always snaked around Tom as if hunting prey.

MELINDA: Why, he attracts them!

HORACE: But he doesn't attract flies, thank goodness. What he does attract is always a worthy woman, I have to admit. If the lady across the way, who we met at their neighborhood party, has her net out for him, we'll see if he can swim, all right.

MELINDA: Now he's the one with the net this time. I heard a car door.

HORACE: I heard the car, Tom's car.

PETER: Bringing out the rum does it. I'll retire.

EXIT PETER

HORACE: *(To Melinda)* I'll follow very soon; I've had my day, I think.

ENTER TOM AND ROSEMARY

TOM: Mother, Father, Rosemary Abbott, our new neighbor.

HORACE: Yes, Tom, we met at their party. Rosemary, welcome to our home.

ROSEMARY: Thank you, Mr. Lightfoot.

TOM: Rosemary and I went into Atlanta to see a play. It had to do with minorities in the states.

MELINDA: What was the name of the play?

TOM: *To Each His Own*, Mother. And not a word about the Amerindian scattered in patchwork across the country.

HORACE: Well, his demands are so miniscule compared to those of some of the others, perhaps, that—

MELINDA: Oh, Horace!

HORACE: Oh, Horace, she says when I get anywhere near a momentary truth, even. She wants me to stick to celestial matters. Sit down, and tell us what else you've been up to. If you can.

TOM: Well, we can. Rosemary and I seem to be stuck somewhere between Sadalsuud and Saca near the Helix.

HORACE: That's far off.

TOM: Yes, we know. There doesn't seem to be an antidote.

HORACE: There isn't, I tell you.

TOM: I know, Father.

MELINDA: If there were one, we would have a barren planet, I think. Congratulations to both of you, and I wish you well on your journey.

HORACE: A journey it is, Tom, and we wish you both the blessings of the gods. Melinda and I are happy when you are happy, and we will leave you the room, we are both tired. But, tell me, who has Meredith met?

TOM: Oh, well, who is Meredith likely to meet? He really moves around down in Atlanta. That fellow travels in different company and I wish him the best. I love Meredith and Paul like brothers.

HORACE: Goodnight.

MELINDA: To you both.

EXIT HORACE AND MELINDA, RIGHT

ROSEMARY: You have a lovely mother and father. It's easy to see I could love them like my own.

TOM: Just don't try to surpass my love for them; it's unsurpassable.

ROSEMARY: I start with my love for you.

TOM: I'll meet and raise you.

ROSEMARY: What, you love yourself, it sounds like!

TOM: How could I love you unless I did? *(Spying the decanter)* Look, rum.

ROSEMARY: And so?

TOM: Some?

ROSEMARY: Little.

TOM: *(Pouring)* Thimble.

ROSEMARY: Thanks.

TOM: Welcome.

ROSEMARY: Tom.

TOM: Yes.

ROSEMARY: *(She drinks)* Love.

TOM: Yes?

ROSEMARY: Words.

TOM: Impractical.

ROSEMARY: Why?

TOM: Barriers.

ROSEMARY: Really?

TOM: Right *(He drinks)*

ROSEMARY: Hand.

TOM: *(Taking her hand)* Warm.

ROSEMARY: *(She drinks)* Hot!

TOM: Why?

ROSEMARY: Guess.

TOM: Can't. *(He drinks)*

ROSEMARY: Try.

TOM: Flashes?

ROSEMARY: Idiot!

TOM: Blood.

ROSEMARY: Correct.

TOM: Heaven.

ROSEMARY: Knows.

TOM: What?

ROSEMARY: All. *(She drinks)*.

TOM: *(He drinks.)* Really.

ROSEMARY: Quite.

TOM: Rosemary,

ROSEMARY: Yes?

TOM: Hand *(Reaching for her other hand)*

ROSEMARY: Yes. *(Providing her hand)*

TOM: More.

ROSEMARY: What?

TOM: All!

ROSEMARY: Finally!!

TOM: Get it?

ROSEMARY: Uh-hm.

TOM: Yes.

ROSEMARY: Yes.

TOM: Finally!!

ROSEMARY: Yes.

TOM: I'll get the car.

ROSEMARY: Please.

TOM: Then—

ROSEMARY: Then?

TOM: Then—

ROSEMARY: Go!

> EXIT TOM *left. A moment later we hear an automobile start,* AND EXIT ROSEMARY. *Beat and* ENTER MEREDITH *and* ESTELLE *from the RIGHT.*

MEREDITH: Neat, eh?

ESTELLE: This all yours?

MEREDITH: You bet.

ESTELLE: Criminy, this is something. You got your nerve, playing the poor Indian with me. This is something. *(We hear Tom's car leave.)*

MEREDITH: Looka the books.

ESTELLE: You read all those? Hey, hey, wait now. Just you wait one minute. This is a put up. You maybe read a role or two of toilet paper but not nothing like this—hey, Winston Churchill. You read that?

MEREDITH: Sure I read it. You think I look at the cartoons or something?

ESTELLE: What! Cartoons in *The History of the English Speaking People*?!

MEREDITH: Yup, political cartoons. Try page two sixty-seven.

ESTELLE: All right. I will. *(Finding the page)* You're not smothering me. Yike! There it is, a cartoon as sure as—

MEREDITH: It's my favorite. Shows France in a negligee; I always think of France like that.

ESTELLE: *(Melting)* Then you do own all this. Criminy.

MEREDITH: Told you I did. I may not use it much, but it's mine, all right. Years ago I decided not to wear it out too quick and took a neat little pad in the back. Keep it nice, I thought.

ESTELLE: My god, you could have a woman in every room!

MEREDITH: Well, I have had. But now I just want you, Estelle.

ESTELLE: Yeah, me and the rest of Atlanta, I bet. Fishy.

MEREDITH: Right, fish love.

ESTELLE: Slimy.

MEREDITH: Ooie, just like. Let's go swim.

ESTELLE: Oh, you got a pool?

MEREDITH: Nope, not what I had in mind. Come on. Wait. A decanter. Glasses. I forgot, I had the maid put them out for us.

ESTELLE: You got a maid, too? I'll bet she gets her hits.

MEREDITH: *(Pouring)* One for you, one and a half for me. *(They drink)*

ESTELLE: That's good stuff. I'll have another.

MEREDITH: Oh, no. Too much bloats you, makes you big. I'd never get a ring on your finger.

ESTELLE: Well, ain't you cheap! All this and another drink raises a stink. But I suppose people with all this must bend the buck someplace. Where do you stay, a room in one of the wings? You got wings, no?

MEREDITH: *(Mimics a bird with his arms)*

ESTELLE: Yeah. Well, I'll have that drink anyway. *(Meredith pours with resignation)* You own this and have to drive me here on a motorscooter! I don't get it.

MEREDITH: Mystery man. *(Smiles)* I heard a noise; we gotta go. Drink.

ESTELLE: What?!

MEREDITH: Drink.

ESTELLE: Here's to us, Sitting Bull. *(Drinks)* Where to, now?

MEREDITH: My pad, over the garage. *(He pulls her out)*

EXIT MEREDITH AND ESTELLE. BEAT AND ENTER PETER

PETER: *(Looks around, curiously, addresses space)* You don't sleep and the house begins to crack and bark to make sure you don't. Old timbers, old everything, old bones, old memories. *(Turns to the picture over the fireplace)* Marie, there is only one thing we do for sure. We begin it all over again. Every new generation of the wolf is the same, needs to keep safe, needs to keep warm, needs his health , needs to hunt, needs to kill. We are on a biological merry-go-round. I loved you more than I knew. Now I know.

EXIT PETER

SCENE FIVE

A few days later, Scene the front of the house again as in Scene One. Two Negro people, one male and one female, knock on the Lightfoot front door. The garden is empty. Horace attends.

JOE: Good morning, sir, we're missionaries for the God of Light Church and we'd like to have a moment of your time, if you have it.

HORACE: I have a moment.

JOE: Is God in your heart, sir? I mean, does He dwell within you? I start you out with that, kind of, because if He's not within, we'd waste your time and ours, sir. Is He within?

HORACE: I would never want you to waste your time, sir.

TIKI: Oh, glory.

JOE: Glory to God, sir. We're canvassing the neighborhood for the church summer camp which does so much good—I wish you could see it. They have games, bible school and more games and comradeship and bible study in an outdoor atmosphere that does them nothing but good, sir. Unfortunately, this coming summer we find ourselves short of funds to do this good deed, and we come to you in the spirit of God, sir, to lend a hand for this good cause.

HORACE: I see.

JOE: I think you do, sir, and it does my heart good and the good lord blesses you.

HORACE: Oh, does he?

JOE: He does, indeed. But I have yet to learn your name, sir.

HORACE: Fair enough, and I have yet to learn yours.

JOE: Forgive me: This is Miss Tikunda, and I am Josef Ramundilassi.

HORACE: What odd names. Are you Americans?

TIKI: We are African Americans.

JOE: Our church is black, as you may have guessed, sir.

HORACE: Yes, and the church denomination?

JOE: Church of the God of Light, I think you mean.

HORACE: No, I mean it's nationality.

JOE: Why, it's African American, of course.

HORACE: I think you say that you are African American and that your church is African American, and I surmise that you may cater to African American children, which would be understandable, to go learn and play in the woods you have secured somewhere in America, no? Do I put that well?

JOE: Yes.

TIKI: But if you impute that all the children are African Americans, you are wrong. Some are white.

HORACE: You mean Caucasian.

TIKI: I do. All attend in the name of God and are treated equally. It's a church summer camp, not a detainment center.

HORACE: Oh, I surely have no question of that, but I hear that you are Africans first and American last. Were you born here?

TIKI: *(Making to go)* Come on, Joe.

JOE: No, wait a minute, Tiki. I think the man is just in search of who we are. Yessir, we were both born here; Tiki in Chicago and me in Atlanta. Both of us are of African descent.

HORACE: Sir, I am of Indian descent, still an American. I come of the land I proclaim mine.

TIKI: I told you we should go. We didn't come here to find out who we are.

HORACE: Do you come from or have you been to Africa?

JOE: No.

HORACE: *(To Tiki)* You?

TIKI: No, no.

HORACE: You have nationality here?

JOE: Yes, we both do.

HORACE: Well, then, you can't hold paper there, it's illegal to be a national here and there together, you know.

TIKI: Joe, I'm goin'!!

HORACE: But, I'm confused, you are seeking funds for a first African and last American church summer camp. I would understand you have already sought funds in Africa and only come to me as necessity dictates.

TIKI: *(Leaving)* I'm gone, Joe.

JOE: So, go! What on earth are you trying to tell me, man?

EXIT WOMAN

HORACE: I am trying to tell you that your naturalization is over, long gone. Be more cohesive and less divisive. We are a beautiful nation with many people of different aspect, sir. Deliver your-self up to America and keep your background as I keep mine.

JOE: I know, I know, I don't know why we do it. I'd rather be just American, too. A feeling of belonging, I guess you'd call it.

RE-ENTER TIKI

TIKI: Joe, you still with that crazy Indian? Come on!

JOE: Tiki, I got more out of this crazy Indian in two minutes than I got out of you in the last two years! I'll be with you.

TIKI: For Godssake, Joe!! *(Pleading)*

JOE: Amen to that, Tiki.

TIKI: Aw, go mess yourself.

EXIT TIKI

JOE: No, sir, I go with what you say. That's cool, all right. I don't lose any pride when I call myself American.; I add to it. Come to think, I've already integrated with religion, with morality, I drive the same make car, wear the same cloth clothes, speak American, eat American, sleep in peace in America, work here and chase women here because I'm a single man. So what the hell! I can't be Argentinean, can I?! What the hell! Where'd that woman go? God bless you, man, and *(Offering an envelope)* send me a check for the kids, will you?

EXIT JOE

SCENE SIX

*Again in the home, as in scene four. High daytime, a bright sun perme-
ating the living room. Present are Horace, Melinda, Father Coughlin and
Maude Abbott, Rosemary's mother. They have just finished tea and
polite conversation.*

HORACE: Well, Father Coughlin and Mrs. Abbott, I'm glad you
enjoyed Melinda's tea and I would like to ask now the purpose
of our pleasant get-together. Since we hadn't seen one another,
Mrs. Abbott, since your fine neighborhood greeting it's our
pleasure to have you here and certainly our pleasure to have
you, Father.

MAUDE: Kind of you, Mr. Lightfoot. We enjoyed having you and
Melinda and Tom, of course, and that's where Rosemary and
Tom first met, I suppose.

MELINDA: No, he told me they had met before when Rosemary had
made her invitation here. Tom can be a bit awkward at large
gatherings.

MAUDE: Well, that fits, then. She was gone from the house for the
longest time that night. Rosemary is a headstrong girl.

MELINDA: I hope there is no problem.

COUGHLIN: None, whatever, I'm sure, Mrs. Lightfoot. The two are in love, it seems, and are having good times together, very naturally. Where in this world can we find two other people occupied with equally important matters? Heads of state would like to claim the kind of harmony they find in one another.

HORACE: True, I think. The greatest composure marriage can retain is some memory of that first unsettling but harmonious meeting. Hard to do, surely, but such a bliss.

MAUDE: It seems you've done it, Mr. Lightfoot.

HORACE: I try, is all.

COUGHLIN: I understand Tom to be a very bright young man, and I think I've perceived a—well, a driven character in Rosemary. One might call the combination an Abraham and Mary Lincoln one.

HORACE: Well, Tom compared to Abraham Lincoln, Melinda. Maybe we raised a significant son, after all.

MELINDA: We did whether he gets compared to Mr. Lincoln or not, Horace.

COUGHLIN: If they marry, it will be a blessed union. Two beautiful people with the world before them: He a student of the heavens with one eye on Venus and the other on God, she the loveliest opal in the grand city museum enclosing God within her. I would love to marry them, myself.

MELINDA: If they marry, yes, I think it would be generous of you, sir.

COUGHLIN: Well, I understand he has proposed, Mrs. Lightfoot.

MELINDA: Has she accepted?

COUGHLIN: I don't know.

MAUDE: Not to my knowledge.

HORACE: Then there's no problem, is there, till the stuff's in the fan, so to speak.

COUGHLIN: There could be the problem of running off or pregnancy, or who knows what.

HORACE: Or there could be the problem of their dancing in my daffodils in the front garden, I suppose, a problem I'd have no answer for except to replant. Why are we finding problems before they exist?

MAUDE: Well, we would rather find them now and have answers than be confounded by their existence, don't you think?

COUGHLIN: Precisely, Maude, better to plan then be caught empty-handed. These are two exemplary people who, I think, would condone our concern. Don't you agree, Mrs. Lightfoot?

HORACE: As well as I think I know our son, I'm not sure he'd relish all this.

MELINDA: But I think the Father and Mrs. Abbott surely have Tom's and Rosemary's welfare in mind.

HORACE: *(Relenting)* I'm, sure they have. I took exception to nothing, really. I find myself too quick to the defense of our son; there may be problems, of course, and I may be the last of those who see them.

COUGHLIN: There is only one apparent problem so far, to my mind. There is the question of Tom's religion, or his practice of it, and the denomination practiced by Rosemary. We haven't seen Tom in Rosemary's church, and that leads us to questioning, you see.

HORACE: I knew it.

COUGHLIN: What did you know?

HORACE: A hitch, just a hitch.

COUGHLIN: But, Mr. Lightfoot, there is no hitch until we find the rope in such a knot we can't deal with it.

HORACE: That's true, all right.

COUGHLIN: May I ask your son's preference?

HORACE: In what, please?

COUGHLIN: Why, the practice of his religion.

HORACE: Oh, dear, Melinda, hasn't mankind been here before? What did he do, then? Did he answer and take the consequences or prevaricate and go home without a scratch? Well, I'll venture honesty. Tom loves art and science, and now, Rosemary. He sees God in a rock, in a valley, in a lady slipper in that valley, in a mountain and in celestial bodies. That's his religion.

COUGHLIN: Does he ever see God in Church?

HORACE: I don't call him to account for his days off work.

COUGHLIN: He never watches celestial bodies on a Sunday?

HORACE: I would imagine so; he saw Rosemary last Sunday.

COUGHLIN: Hardly what I meant, sir.

HORACE: I know. My apology, Father.

MAUDE: I think Mr. Lightfoot is not so inclined to plan with us as you may think, Father. I believe he may be tired of cooperating with us, and I wouldn't want to make an angry neighbor of him. Shall we just let things be bye-the-bye for now?

COUGHLIN: I think that's well taken, Maude, but—as your priest—I would like to come away with one more little piece of information, for your sake. With your permission, Mr. Lightfoot.

HORACE: I'm curious, sir.

MELINDA: I, also.

COUGHLIN: Is Tom a Christian, Mr. Lightfoot?

HORACE: I would say so.

COUGHLIN: No, I mean, does he accept the holy trinity of God, the Father and the Holy Ghost?

HORACE: I've never asked him that.

COUGHLIN: I see.

HORACE: The ground beneath our feet is God, is it not, Father?

COUGHLIN: Does he think so?

HORACE: I hear him coming in the side door; you may ask him yourself.

ENTER TOM AND ROSEMARY

ROSEMARY: Mother! And Father Coughlin! You surprise the devil out of me, but I suppose that's a good thing.

MAUDE: It is a good thing, Rosemary, but we have already discussed the devil out of you—and out of Tom, too, for that matter. Father Coughlin and I came to do just that and we have almost completed the job.

COUGHLIN: Rosemary, it was your mother's desire to have us come and help prepare the way for both of you in the event you were anticipating holy marriage.

ROSEMARY: Mother! I confided that to you.

MAUDE: No confidence was broken when Father Coughlin heard it. He is our priest, and your family priest is the securest repository for personal information you can imagine, dear.

ROSEMARY: Oh, yes. I see that.

TOM: Dad, what is this? I don't even begin to understand.

HORACE: It's a—it's a planning session, I guess, wherein your lives are being qualified for the times ahead wherever they may lead. Is that fair, Father?

COUGHLIN: I suppose so, if you look at it that way. But let me add that Mrs. Abbott simply wants to secure a happy future for Rosemary, which I'm sure is entirely possible once we understand where we are in the matter.

TOM: Well, then, where are we?

COUGHLIN: We are attempting to find out, as I said, Tom. I am trying to find, really, what alignment you may have with Rosemary's faith toward the most propitious of possible futures for you both.

TOM: Well, Father, we haven't had time to disagree on the subject.

COUGHLIN: Don't you think you might at some time in the future? You see, the fact that love is blind could cause you a rude awakening sometime.

TOM: You want to take the blinders off?

COUGHLIN: Well, no, but expand your vision a bit, maybe.

TOM: My vision, Father, comes from my father and my mother. To them I owe the stars. Literally. My father's vision guided me through the slavery of childhood and into learning. He provided the questions, he provided the books. This woman *(pointing to his mother)* fed me when I was too new to the contraptions of the table to understand. She gave me the vision of self-help and self-care. She gave me the warmth of her body when I hurt. I've had the best of vision poured into me. I can only trust to my own uses of those visions not to put discouragement into my or anyone else's life.

MAUDE: Father Coughlin is here to help, Tom, not to challenge you.

TOM: You're the mother of my most concentrated love, Mrs. Abbott, and I honor you that.

COUGHLIN: All we need to know, Tom, is whether you think your faith will be, till eternity, one that is compatible with Rosemary's.

TOM: Is that all?

COUGHLIN: That is all.

TOM: What is hers?

COUGHLIN: She is high Episcopal.

TOM: I am low Indian.

COUGHLIN: I don't understand. Do you think them compatible?

TOM: *(Quietly)* Hell, yes.

COUGHLIN: I believe he makes a joke, Maude.

TOM: Now, whether this compatibility will last 'til eternity, I can't tell you, really, not knowing the duration of your eternity. Is it the duration of one or both of us or the duration of the world? If the latter, I have no way of knowing. If the former, then, too, I can't speculate with time. We may both alter our opinions and turn heretics.

HORACE: Tom, you are being impolite to guests.

TOM: My apology to you both for my anger.

MAUDE: I believe we have almost learned what we came for, and I must go take care of a hungry husband. Horace and Melinda, I thank you for your time and tea. And to the two lovers, my own love. Come, Father.

COUGHLIN: With you, Maude, and many thanks to our hosts for time and tea, yes. And my love to both lovers, also.

EXIT MRS. ABBOTT AND FATHER COUGHLIN

TOM: My apology to all of us here, too. I lost it.

HORACE: Yes, you did, Tom. But if I'm to be guilty of the wisdom you accuse me of, I understand.

TOM: It was a damned inquisition, something out of the thirteenth century without a change of form, even. It was sickening. Rosemary, am I being unfair?

ROSEMARY: No, they are the ones who were unfair. I'm embarrassed for them.

MELINDA: But I understand their concern, too. They want an agreeable marriage for both of you.

ROSEMARY: But I haven't even said yes to him, yet! What happens after?!

TOM: I'll tell you what happens after if you tell me now. I've waited long enough.

ROSEMARY: Yes, yes and yes, again. You knew you had a lock on that when you asked me.

TOM: Now, what happens after is—*(He kisses her)* I kiss the witch.

HORACE: Bravo, Tom, well done.

MELINDA: Happiness to you both. *(Rosemary offers herself first to Melinda, then Horace. They embrace)*

ROSEMARY: *(To Tom)* But what is low Indian, now?

HORACE: Good question, Tom.

MELINDA: Your father and I have chores. Will you stay to dinner, Rosemary?

ROSEMARY: Thank you, Melinda.

EXIT HORACE AND MELINDA

TOM: What did they mean, your mother and that cloaked soul hunter? What right do they have to search out my faith? Fancy your mother suddenly with a turnip for a nose. Such a sweet woman turned public investigator. Why she?! And why him?! He bore into me like an augur bit. Next thing they want to know, I'll be obliged to drop my pants.

ROSEMARY: I'm sure my mother was being protective. Why, I'm not sure. But Father Coughlin—He was—

TOM: Wasn't he, though? Hey, for dogged determination and nailed to the point, for the most studied language and polished diction, he scored at the university level. He was an eloquent bore.

ROSEMARY: Then why are you angry? My mother is innocent of what she did. She followed the father, is all.

TOM: No, she brought him, not the reverse.

ROSEMARY: Tom, love, what is low Indian?

TOM: Just that.

ROSEMARY: Just what?

TOM: There is no other description of it; it defines itself.

ROSEMARY: Then, how am I supposed to know it, not knowing it? I need something.

TOM: It's a Chickasaw thing.

ROSEMARY: Oh, dear, too secular. Please.

TOM: Low Indian, my sweet, is a kind of terrestrial thing finding God in all things: In the ground under our feet which is the decomposition of stone, in the air we breathe, in war, in peace. Your religion says that God is everywhere, mine particularizes that. They could never be more compatible.

ROSEMARY: I see.

TOM: The little differences will be erased by love.

ROSEMARY: Oh, Tom, I so wanted our faiths to fit together as we do. I hope they do. We're so rich, we two. Look what we have behind us: My good parents and yours, both rich in what they gave to us, despite my mother today. Look what we have ahead: Two faiths that bring us to fruition together. It's like looking at the sky and seeing the sun above one horizon and the moon above the other, separate but together, brilliant and dull and at another time dull and brilliant, still together. How you like that for a skyward picture?

TOM: God, I love you.

ROSEMARY: Well, you should. You recently said that in order to love me, you must first love yourself. Well, I also love myself in order to love you. That love we have of ourselves, it seems to me, is the vast outflowing we release when we find a vessel to contain it. Does that seem right? You are my vessel, I'm yours then. And what a vessel you are, my love.

TOM: It takes one to know one.

ROSEMARY: And it takes one more, maybe more than one, to know how knowing those two are of one another. Those are our parents, whose wisdom of us is so comforting. My father says I am a peony, colorful in the round. Does that add?

TOM: Oh, I'm sure. I would never contest the wisdom of a parent.

ROSEMARY: And, now, it is described in our histories that the brave is the hunter and the squaw the forager. What about that? You hunt the skies for something new in Andromeda, you've told me, and the woods and beaches with a binocular for an unexpected species of bird. Well, the hunt goes on then. I will forage in the markets for the berry with the magic love potion and stuff you to bloating with it. And so goes the forage. Then we will make our own tribe.

TOM: Ah, something needs a moment here.

ROSEMARY: What?

TOM: I love you with every drop of blood in me, Rosemary, but I have no need to prove it with a tribe.

ROSEMARY: No children, Tom?

TOM: No thought of them for now, is all. I'll call it my unwillingness to dilute my attention. It's intense, and I intend to keep it that way.

ROSEMARY: But for how long?

TOM: A while, at least.

ROSEMARY: Tom, Thomas, my love, you are striking at my faith. Family is a given. In the name of God, it is a right-of-way in marriage, a reason itself for the existence of marriage.

TOM: And love?

ROSEMARY: What do you mean?

TOM: No, what do you mean? Are children an expedient of marriage? Is marriage an expedient of love? If so, I wonder where cause and effect might take us.

ROSEMARY: It would be unusual for a marriage not to have family.

TOM: Unusual, yes; unworthy, no. A true Indian never overbreeds his hunting ground. He knows the price of overpopulation; it's death.

ROSEMARY: Then you mean no tribe ever.

TOM: I may. Dear Rosemary, I want to study, I want to learn and allow you to do both, also. There are so many warm nights ahead for us and revealing days. I want the world to continue opening herself to us so that we may accrue meanings close to our potential. Children would occupy us to an extent we could regret.

ROSEMARY: My God in heaven, I am hearing such frightening things that I'm not believing them. Why am I afraid?

TOM: The fear is yours, not mine, Rosemary. I had hoped to avoid this until—

ROSEMARY: And then leave me barren in marriage, or what?

TOM: Marriage without children is hardly barren by definition. A barren marriage is one in which the principals are barren. And if that's the case, it would be best that no children were had, I think. Let's test the water before we even think of swimming in it. Rosemary? There is no greater love than mine for you. Rosemary.

ROSEMARY: Well, I'm stunned. Like a little old sea bass by a manta ray. Such surprise. I'll just turn on my side and play dead. When the mean old ray has gone off, I'll recover and go my way, maybe.

TOM: That's ominous, and I'll disregard it.

ROSEMARY: Oh, Tom, what fear grows in me! The yacht has sprung a leak and the water is cold and dark. And I don't want to be a little old sea bass.

TOM: It is nothing more and no less than our first issue.

ROSEMARY: Issue! This is merely an issue? This is glass breaking, the shards are in a cataract here. And I'm bloody. Mind me, Tom, I'm bloody.

TOM: I love you bloody.

ROSEMARY: Well, I don't! How did something so easily intrude itself that now we look at one another as strangers. What's happening here? The world is becoming so damn foreign.

TOM: Maybe it's the speed at which we were both sent careening through the world. Were we careless? No doubt, but we were running with the pack, then ahead of it, then way ahead. Freedom, freedom, freedoom, freedoom.

ROSEMARY: Also, I'm sure. But there are no ticker-tapes waiting for us on Broadway if there is no tribe. The color of everything is changed now and, in fact, black peeks in. Why can't we keep the black out, Tom? Tell me you love me, again.

TOM: It's past love. I venerate you. I see you dancing on the highest church spire in America, balanced and having the time of your life. If you fall, I'll catch you.

ROSEMARY: I won't fall.

TOM: Je t'aime.

ROSEMARY: Oh.

TOM: Ich liebe dich.

ROSEMARY: Oh, again.

TOM: It's an international love.

ROSEMARY: Oh, Tom.

TOM: Don't deprive us both of our happiness for a single idea, Rosemary.

ROSEMARY: But what an idea, you must admit.

TOM: I do, but I admit my idea is just as singular as yours and has the world population to support it.

ROSEMARY: The world population? Would you clear that up for me, please?

TOM: Yes, multiplication is adding little people at a staggering rate and I question whether quantity lives will humble the quality life shortly. It would seem so. If the poet and composer have no room to idle in the woods, what kinds of stuff will they feed us?

ROSEMARY: Do you mean to tell me that your hesitance to have children is caused by the world's population? Tom, do you tell me that?!

TOM: Yes, love, we are both Indian; we should understand that.

ROSEMARY: But we—

TOM: No, we're not past the need to contain ourselves. Before, it was the need to regulate a territory, now it's the need to regulate the world—a larger territory. No difference, but the size. It has gone from "save the buffalo" to "save his entire range;" from "save the queen" to "save her court." You hear the tiresome caterwauling of the environmentalist, don't you? Well, it's true as well as tiresome. It is a truth aimed to tire you by its weight. You, a Cherokee, protecting your territory, should know about the seriousness of diminishing land. You lost yours to the breeding of the Caucasian. Lost, Rosemary. Lost to numbers!

ROSEMARY: Do you think we should stop meeting in the bedroom, Tom?

TOM: I don't see why, perhaps meet more often, but for love—not the implementation of another life, another decimal point.

ROSEMARY: But if we abstain, and all good souls abstain, and the derelict and the ignorant flourish, then what, my Chickasaw love?

TOM: I have no answer for eventualities, just the present. Everything begins here.

ROSEMARY: Oh, God, I'm lost. Here I am in a vast field of rough grasses, surrounded by insurmountable, sheer, mountains of such size that passing them is impossible and the only sun I know is shielded by them. It's not a pretty picture.

TOM: We can survive it.

ROSEMARY: Perhaps you can; I'm not so sure of myself. If it means giving up my womanhood—

TOM: It means nothing like that! You have your womanhood, it's yours! Motherhood is another hat. You wear the hat of

womanhood exquisitely, and I love it on you. Don't shroud it
with the mother's!

ROSEMARY: Oh, Tom, I never thought that, on entering marriage, I
would shroud myself with motherhood.

TOM: I'm failing to be clear.

ROSEMARY: No, I think you're quite clear.

TOM: It would help if I could believe that.

ROSEMARY: That would help you, would it?

TOM: Yes.

ROSEMARY: And help for me? Where do I find that?

TOM: I don't understand.

ROSEMARY: This is unimaginable to me.

TOM: Rosemary, what is—?

ROSEMARY: The dumb show goes on. The miscarriage is enough; the
midwife stands and watches the mother bleed. Thumbs go
down; she'll kill me. Oh, how marvelous is this sport of bear
and deliver, venture and lose. Am I prolix?

TOM: You stole a march; you'll have to let me catch you.

ROSEMARY: Oh, Tom, I don't know any longer if I want you to!

TOM: I despise hearing that. It disposes of me. It leaves a shadow behind, maybe a shadow. Maybe not even a memory. Why would you suddenly have an idea like that? Children? Is that— Rosemary, I want the freedom to love you! I have no other purpose in life but to love you!

ROSEMARY: You've struck at my faith, Tom.

TOM: It's not even yours, Rosemary! It's your elders and those of history before you. It's their faith, held during a time with different needs and requirements. Times do change, my sweet, oh, do they change. And if they didn't, man could stop thinking because last year's thoughts would still apply. We should meet our time head on, seize it, and understand. I haven't struck at your faith, Rosemary, I've only found that I have one idea about something and you have another. Love will guide us to a conclusion.

ROSEMARY: An idea, only, you say?

TOM: Yes, I say so. An idea between us, ours, which we need to adjust to our lives. Yours and mine. Should I allow Schopenhauer my view of women? Well, it would destroy our love. I'd go to bachelorhood forever and you to maidenhood.

ROSEMARY: I want to be free of all this.

TOM: No, Rosemary, that would give you dominion over it. We are in the world, not over it. Take my hand.

ROSEMARY: No, Tom.

TOM: To share the feel of belonging.

ROSEMARY: No, please.

TOM: Together.

ROSEMARY: I can no more do that than look at you, Tom.

TOM: Another cut. You seem to bleed and die while still thrashing round with your own sword.

ROSEMARY: I do hate this.

TOM: Rosemary, you mean far more to me than this; please make me the same to you. That's what we need, kind of an equalization of values. I feel my value to you is a lot diminished, and I could never live with that.

ROSEMARY: It is diminished.

TOM: My God, it's not. I won't hear that.

ROSEMARY: It's as though with your diminishing me, I must return the insult. I detest all this; it doesn't seem a compliment to either of us.

TOM: What do I say?

ROSEMARY: Nothing.

TOM: Your elders are punishing me through you. I see them racking me.

ROSEMARY: You may see what you like, I suppose.

TOM: Well, that's what I see. And I hope tomorrow will be another day.

ROSEMARY: No, it won't be. It will be night.

EXIT ROSEMARY

———————————————

Scene Seven

The same scene as six. Weeks later, high in the afternoon. Present are Peter and Melinda.

PETER: Yes, I saw the change this morning. After nearly a month of dragging his body with him, he steps out and is working like a beaver. It's a relief to see him back to normal. He was even beginning to depress me.

MELINDA: I hope—I only hope it's real, Father. It seems strange to step out of one behavior into another so easily.

PETER: Oh, it could be the impatience of the body, simply, refusing to be geared to a sluggish mentality any longer. Everything quickens when that happens.

MELINDA: I hope it's more.

PETER: No visit from the woman who shuns him, nor does he visit her. I'd say the whole thing is over the edge and under water, and best done with, probably.

MELINDA: Who knows?

PETER: No one knows, and no one still knows what happened. He's a good young man you should be proud of. Licks his own wounds and survives it. I love him, as I would want to.

MELINDA: Father, you'd love to see the boy out throwing spears at buffalo and shooting arrows at deer. You'd love to see him in skins and a headdress.

PETER: You are the most misinformed daughter I have. The only one, but still the most misinformed. I think I've come a long way from my origins and with my origins.

MELINDA: Of course, and I'm proud of you. The day I accepted Horace, I got twice the number of hawks I had counted on.

PETER: When you got me, Melinda, you got the eagle.

MELINDA: Oh, tell me about it.

ENTER TOM

TOM: Did Meredith come in here? He was just outside the door a minute ago behind the truck.

MELINDA: No, Tom.

TOM: That rascal.

ENTER MEREDITH

MEREDITH: That's right, rascal, you've got it. Where's Meredith? Well, the rascal was in the truck lashing down the scope for delivery. Standing outside wondering where I am won't get it. Calling me rascal nails it, though. Want to know why? I finally took a woman. Yeah. Little ol' Estelle. You'll meet her. I'll be moving out to a new pad in a day or two, but I hope you'll keep my spot open here for me. I'm not about to be divorcing you before I'm even married, you know. Couldn't think of leaving the folks I'm beholden to. You can congratulate me now.

MELINDA: Oh, Meredith, of course we wish you all the best.

MEREDITH: You, Tom?

TOM: *(with resignation)* Yes, Meredith.

MEREDITH: You sure?

TOM: I'm sure.

MEREDITH: I'm so convinced it hurts, but I'll get Paul and we'll go.

EXIT MEREDITH

MELINDA: You have us very confused today, Tom. We were used to favoring your melancholy and then you seem to be over it so suddenly we hardly know which face to show to you.

TOM: Dear Mother, show me the one you're most at home with, that's all.

PETER: That's not much help.

TOM: I know. It's pretty unfeeling of me to retire everything. For some time you've known that Rosemary and I were not meeting. For that time you let me be as quiet as I chose, and I thank you. I might say that she and I are over a hump, but that it divided us. It was a great shock to both. Understandable. Damnable, but acceptable to me, now, and no doubt to her, also, since she's silent, too. I can breathe again, and I like breathing. I can almost feel again, almost.

A TRUCK STARTS AND DRIVES OFF OUTSIDE

MELINDA: (Going to him) Oh, my son, Thomas, you've had a bad turn, and I'm sorry it seems finished for you.

TOM: The finishing is the curing, Mother.

PETER: Be sure, Tom, the wisdom of owls is in the waiting.

TOM: But they wait game, Grandfather. I just look for the things I had before, two steps past gaming, I hope. I want to get back to that up there and the use of a glass in the field. I want to take a step past all my yesterdays.

PETER: Good boy, then. I'll take you to Brasstown Bald next Spring for the chestnut-sided warbler.

TOM: You're on. Although you spoil things, don't you, when you point out a four-and-a-half inch bird in canopy without a binocular?

PETER: Prism binoculars are expensive. If I needed one, I'd buy it from you.

MELINDA: Are you sure, son?

TOM: Yes, Mother, sure. I loved Rosemary, she loved me, and then it rained. We took a soaking.

MELINDA: As you say.

TOM: No more pain; it's dead. I—me, too.

MELINDA: Was it your Indian blood?

TOM: No, no, she had her own, even, a Cherokee.

MELINDA: Then I'm sorry it failed.

PETER: See here, Tom, there's another fine play in Atlanta and I'll stir my money bucket and treat the family to seats. What do you say?

THE BELL RINGS. Melinda attends

Say it before something trivial interrupts us.

TOM: Sold, sir.

ENTER MAUDE AND ROSEMARY AND MELINDA

MAUDE: I am sorry to intrude. I am downright fearful of intruding, I should say. The last time I was here I was soon made aware I had come with the wrong company, and so this time I hope I have come with the right one.

MELINDA: You are certainly welcome in our home, Maude.

MAUDE: And hoping I have the right company this time. I think I have to make a little speech. She is in no shape for it.

ROSEMARY: Mother—

MAUDE: She has been sick for near a month now. She has asked questions about protocol that I have never experienced before and so had no answer for. I am not a librarian to love. I told her all I could tell her; confront the horse who threw you and ask why.

TOM: The horse who threw her, Mrs. Abbott, was tired of the spur.

MAUDE: Let me change approaches, then. We both wonder why the nest fell from the tree.

TOM: I don't think I'll touch that.

MAUDE: Is it because eggs wouldn't occupy it? I hear so.

MELINDA: I think I'm not in the same season with you, Maude.

PETER: Well, who wants all his eggs in one nest, anyway? Ask any cowbird.

TOM: Oh, the ornithology here! But the sparrow in the streets is not the song or the vesper sparrow. It's a finch with a flinch at the truth, a liar. There was never any nest, I tell you, only a thought. And then a wholescale war. But no nest.

MAUDE: Dear me, do I need to find another figure of speech?

TOM: You need to find your way home, more than likely. It would be the clever thing to do.

MELINDA: Tom, you will apologize to Mrs. Abbott while I stand here.

PETER: And while I leave.

EXIT PETER

TOM: Yes ma'm. Mrs. Abbott, it was unkind of me to suggest you find your way home. I'll find it for you.

MELINDA: I hope I have not heard what I heard.

TOM: Mother, I have too many things to do today to listen to another Quisling, one who encourages cooperation at any price. I would rather take the time to show her home, with or without her slave girl.

MAUDE: Well, come along, Rosemary. Mr. Lightfoot is in a dizzy spell, thinking how busy he is. Come along. No, wait. You stay, and I'll find my way home. I can do it, and maybe the treatment will improve if I'm gone. See to it.

EXIT MAUDE

MELINDA: *(To Tom)* I'm not aware of ever hearing you like this, Tom, and I hope you will apologize.

EXIT MELINDA

TOM: What in hell, Rosemary?

ROSEMARY: What in heaven would be closer to your mother's wish?

TOM: Well, either place, what do you want?

ROSEMARY: I thought we might talk.

TOM: Well, together or while one listens?

ROSEMARY: Please, Tom, I never meant to hurt us. I've been in bed many days, exhausted and depressed for it. I have, I've hurt us both and I take responsibility. Can we discuss it?

TOM: You do, and I'll listen.

ROSEMARY: Mother brought me here with the best intentions, to sound out our love and know its depth, if it had any. She is not a diplomat; she is my mother. You treated her rudely, and not for the first time—but I understand; you were angry with her. Don't be angry with me, Tom. It took all my strength to come here, and I think I came for a good purpose.

TOM: Yes?

ROSEMARY: I can hope so, anyway. *(Fighting a vertigo)* I haven't been well for this, but I can tell you in any condition that I love you. That is rock solid. That's immovable.

TOM: Wait, Rosemary.

ROSEMARY: I have never had such an experience before; it was all encompassing and all fulfilling. It was the richest thing I had ever known. An eclair.

TOM: Edible, you mean.

ROSEMARY: No. Nothing could consume it. It was like—like confronting a great, high, stone wall—so imposing that you could do nothing but lie down in its shade. I succumbed; I thought you did, too. If I was wrong, I have already paid something and will pay more. I—I thought you did, at any rate.

TOM: That's true; I did, Rosemary.

ROSEMARY: I had never felt so full of someone. No one had ever occupied so much room in me. I am not talking physical matters, I am talking the length and breadth of me weighted with another presence. Day and night. Heavy, but rich as a Christmas time eggnog and even more warming. Heavy and heady, both. I wore a crown.

TOM: Thorns?

ROSEMARY: No, of content. My world was full of all the ideas I had ever dreamt for it. Whether my thoughts were of realities or fictions mattered nothing. I'd been mesmerized.

TOM: Oh, cruel fate.

ROSEMARY: If it were cruel, it was the kind of cruelty one seeks and when it's found, won't give it up. A drinker's alcohol, a smoker's tobacco, a lover's love. How easily each becomes a habit and how difficult is riddance.

TOM: Well, it will come.

ROSEMARY: I have no way of knowing that. You can suggest it; I won't think so. You can state that it's so; I still won't know it. You can vow it's so; I won't believe you. I never know a thing before it happens. I suppose that 's why we are either happy with something or unhappy, despite our best expectations for it.

TOM: You have my promise.

ROSEMARY: So soon after I have your promise of love? How reversible can you get? A monk's robe turned inside-out for a devil's dress? Oh, dear Tom, I have your promise. (Beat) Again.

TOM: My word, then.

ROSEMARY: Is that better? Does one improve the other? I think not. I won't take either one that causes me to think I don't love you. I do, so far within me no language can touch it. Oh, I wish now that I could see it as a surface thing and remove it with a towel or cloth. Or like a ring, slip it on and take it off. Like a stocking, like a shoe. But it's the seed of the apple. *(Then, some amused with her image, she smiles weakly)* Take a bite? *(With no response from Tom she apologizes)* I see you're not hungry. But even that doesn't put out love; the flame's inside, Tom. And I can tell you, it burns. There is some old stuff about undying love. No chance for it. In its prime since our beginning, mine hasn't even aged. There is nothing like that, you know. What takes space but is still timeless, what flower, what verse? Only thinking seems to be. Imagine, thought! That's even romantic. Thought changes. If yours of me changed, I would die inside. Because that's where it all is. As I told you. Where it all is. What good, you know, if the seed dies for the apple to remain red? It's only a matter of time, is it not?

TOM: My word and my promise are not good; what will you take?

ROSEMARY: Whatever you will offer.

TOM: I offer that I am no longer in love.

ROSEMARY: That's more than I had hoped for.

TOM: A matter of issues.

ROSEMARY: Once you said those were negotiable.

TOM: They were, then. There was a time for them before the animation died. Before the night sky lost the depth of its darkness. Day approaches, and after several of those, it snows. Surprising as it is, it's accepted. And one bundles against it, even enjoys the cool.

ROSEMARY: No, Tom.

TOM: Nearly a month went before I could keep my food down. I fought to clear my head, my mind was a cesspool. Finally, though, I understood your objection, and that was that.

ROSEMARY: That was what?

TOM: It was what I needed, to accept your objection.

ROSEMARY: *(Hopefully)* Do you mean, I hope?

TOM: No. It was you. It was some of you I hadn't known. It was a very serious position you took toward the world, toward me, and I wanted it to be otherwise. But was not to be. I probably have yet to learn that I am not going to alert the world to the seriousness of numbering that afflicts us. I must let others be their others, yours included, Rosemary. So, the acceptance.

ROSEMARY: I hear you say that you no longer love me.

TOM: It pays to listen.

ROSEMARY: And to understand?

TOM: I fear so.

ROSEMARY: I am going to be sick. Please do excuse me.

ROSEMARY EXITS RIGHT. TOM SITS. *Several beats.*
PETER ENTERS.

PETER: Tom, I never asked one item of your relationship with that woman, Rosemary, and I am not doing that now—it is not my place—but she's attended to by your mother and sicker than a gull that took down a fish wrong. I once saw that on a bank of the Chattahoochee, and the next morning the gull was on his back. That night a raccoon may have dispatched him, because next morning he was gone. What do you want done?

TOM: Nothing, Grandfather.

PETER: Well, now, I will ask one item—and only one alone: do you love that woman?

TOM: I did love her, yes.

PETER: That answers it, I suppose. I was an embarrassment to my youth. I courted Marie till I was short of breath, and one day she ended my shyness by asking did I love her or did I not. I had two ways to go, I guess, and thank goodness I went with the right answer. Were you shy, Tom?

TOM: No.

PETER: Do you go the right way, Tom?

TOM: I don't know sir.

PETER: Don't punt, boy, play it out.

TOM: Peter, have you ever done a sweat for principle? That is, sacrificed something or even someone for something you believe with all your being?

PETER: I gave up my standing in the Cherokee community to marry Marie. She was a Creek.

TOM: Was it worth it?

PETER: More than. I took the best the Creeks had to offer. When she walked, the blue flag melted beneath her, the beaver built dams for her to bridge water with, and the vireo sang her all day long. That's why he still sings the whole day.

TOM: *(Musing)* You were the Cherokee, she the Creek. Maybe that's a better arrangement. She was the Cherokee.

PETER: You're sounding as distant as a dead man, but you're not dead.

TOM: Do I have to show a skeleton?

PETER: If that's the case, I'm sorry for you. You lost.

TOM: Yes. How long is death, sir?

PETER: Long, Tom, long. Forever.

ENTER MELINDA

MELINDA: I must tell you, Tom, that girl is ill. When she almost passed out, I took her into your bedroom where she's resting.

TOM: Thank you.

MELINDA: That's all, just thank you? You won't go to her?

PETER: *(Near the window)* Well, look here, some children have inherited our front lawn for a game of tag. If I were that young again, I'd catch them all in a minute. *(Melinda and Tom are drawn to the window)*

MELINDA: It's all right; they're below the flowers. My, look at that young thing run.

TOM: Tag. *(We begin to hear lightly the children's voices)*

MELINDA: Yes, tag. You ran like that once.

TOM: Still do, Mother, I still do.

MELINDA: What do you mean?

TOM: But once is enough, maybe.

MELINDA: Oh, then what?

TOM: And enough is enough, is all.

MELINDA: Such nonsense, Tom. I'll go see to that sick girl.

EXIT MELINDA

PETER: And what's enough, Tom?

TOM: I don't know; all. It seems unjust that the common spider weaves a firmer web than we do. *(There is a stifled scream and)*

ENTER HORACE LIGHTFOOT

HORACE: Tom, I think that came from your room.

EXIT TOM

PETER: I have seen it, and I will see it again. If this eagle takes a duck and that eagle takes a ewe, are we to blame the eagles? If this falcon takes an egret, and that falcon takes a songbird, do we blame falcons?

HORACE: We do everything we find purpose for, I suppose, Father, which leaves us on the back side of the moon.

ENTER TOM CARRYING THE BODY OF ROSEMARY

TOM: Done with my own knife! As though my hand on it! Look! My witch is dead, Father! No issue here, anymore, no debate! No voice! I would have loved her to my last bone, had I known. I put out my love, now she does hers. And death to death is fair enough. My mother is in my bed, Father, Rosemary in hers, and there is nothing between us now.

HORACE: Take her to another room, Tom. Then come to me, I want to put my arm around you.

TOM: You'll embrace a dead man, Father.

HORACE: I will have my affection, Son.

EXIT TOM CARRYING ROSEMARY

PETER: Oh, Marie, our time, though sculpted from gold, is gone to dust. Theirs barely dusted, dries, rusts, erodes but will be retold. How brief unhappy histories make the past and lasting story.

———————————

END

———————————